Cheam and Belmont

IN OLD PHOTOGRAPHS

Cheam and Belmont

IN OLD PHOTOGRAPHS

Collected by PATRICIA BERRY

Alan Sutton Publishing Limited
Phoenix Mill · Far Thrupp
Stroud · Gloucestershire

First Published in 1993

Copyright © Patricia Berry, 1993

British Library Cataloguing in Publication Data

Berry, Patricia
  Cheam & Belmont in Old Photographs
  I. Title
  942.192

  ISBN 0-7509-0335-X

Typeset in 9/10 Sabon.
Typesetting and origination by
Alan Sutton Publishing Limited.
Printed in Great Britain by
Redwood Books, Trowbridge.

Contents

The Broadway, Cheam, looking north from the traffic-lights.

Cheam

People have lived in the area now called Cheam for many hundreds of years. Earlier names included Cegeham (the place of wooden stumps), Cheiham, Kaham and Chayham. Under the ancient system of dividing shires into 'hundreds' whose leading citizens assembled at intervals to settle local matters, Cheam was in the hundred of Wallington. Earl Godwin, father of King Harold, had owned much of Surrey but, after his son's defeat in 1066, the conquering William gave the greater part to his own half-brother, Odo.

When, ten years later, William sent forth his commissioners and clerks to 'find out what or how much every landowner holds in land and livestock and its worth', the entry in Domesday recorded that the Archbishop of Canterbury had Cheam himself 'for the supplies of the monks'; that is to say food and grain, and no doubt Friday fish from the stew-ponds, went direct to the abbey kitchens.

Signs of Saxon burials and relics of Roman pottery were unearthed in the vicinity earlier this century, and it is probable that more clues to pre-conquest settlements lie beneath our streets and houses. Such ancient habitations are known to have existed at nearby Ewell and Epsom, and Cheam lies on the same corridor of land. Thanet sand reaches the surface at all three places through a fault in the chalk. Good water from deep wells was obtainable along that line, so small villages grew up from earliest times.

The Domesday entry for Cheam (Ceiha) records enough villagers, cottagers and slaves to suggest a population of 250–300, and also mentions a church. Traces of Norman window arches can still be seen in the south wall of the Lumley chapel, close to the present St Dunstan's church. Within the chapel some brasses and sculpture dating from the fifteenth century, or even earlier, were found. Of a similar date were examples of pottery unearthed in the High Street/Malden Road/Parkside area.

Cheam has a thirteenth-century connection, regarded as 'gospel' in my childhood but now treated with some scepticism. This concerns the origin of the fair held on 15 May every year in Park Road. Whether or not King Henry III or any other sovereign granted a charter, the fair now seems firmly established.

It was King Henry VIII who brought one phase of prosperity to Cheam, though at the expense of an entire village little more than a mile away. His eye fell on the manor house, church and parish of Cuddington and some 1,800 acres of land, and nothing would do but to clear the site and build his new country seat of Nonsuch there. Though the London Road entrance to Nonsuch Park was the favoured approach to the king's fantasy palace, there was a corresponding gateway on the Cheam side, where the curve of the A232 Ewell road at this point still follows the line of the pale (park boundary).

The old king died as Nonsuch was completed, but it became a favourite of his younger daughter Elizabeth, whose visits, involving days of hunting, coursing, banqueting, masques and entertainments, spanned almost fifty years. One of Cheam's oldest surviving houses, Whitehall, or 'the Council House', was standing at this time and was probably known to the queen, though some today cast doubt on the romantic tradition that she used it for an impromptu meeting when urgent state matters arose. The house was not then weatherboarded but timber-framed, like the tiny building now standing in the Broadway, the Old Cottage. That existed then, too, though it was situated farther south.

The Tudor village was concentrated in that area, surrounded by the estates and farmlands of East Cheam Manor (towards Gander Green Lane), Cheam Court Farm (near today's village crossroads) and West Cheam Manor (near the church). Some relics have survived, like the splendid chalk-block wall overlooking the churchyard. We remember others, such as the village pond, by name only (Pond Hill Gardens), but the outline of King Henry's palace can be seen on the badge of Nonsuch High School for Girls.

If one can ignore Cheam's modern streets, with their fury of traffic, and exercise some quiet imagination, a mental picture will emerge of the village's simple road pattern long ago. Many an inhabitant in a lifetime might journey no farther than the next village; those in a position to travel on horseback or by coach might sometimes visit a neighbouring town or even London. The road from Sutton took a westerly line via today's footpath behind St Nicholas's church, Camden, Western and Tate Roads, and Love Lane. Running roughly parallel to Cheam Road it can still be followed. From south to north the tracks that became Sandy Lane and Burdon Lane curved slightly left and continued to the London road at North Cheam via what has now been reinstated as Cheam Park Way, a mere cart track only a generation ago.

Although a St Dunstan's congregation had the dubious distinction of hearing a sermon preached against the evils of the London, Brighton and South Coast Railway, a village like Cheam could not stand on the road to such important places without developing. It was the coming of the railway in 1847, the laying of water mains, beginning in 1863, and the consequent freeing of land for residential building that caused the expansion that has continued ever since.

Sadly the 'old is bad' maxim was upheld and fine old houses that we can only read about are lost. Engravings, photographs and plans of the 1746 parish church, for example, reveal a simple building with a square tower amid ancient tombstones. Lost forever are the eighteenth-century Cheam House, demolished in the early 1920s; the pigeon house of West Cheam Manor, gone at the turn of the century; and Cheam School, Alma Mater of many famous men, a building in the High Street that I can just remember standing empty and awaiting demolition in 1934.

I was brought to live in Cheam when I was only a few days old and grew up believing it to be the best village on earth. Local history did not then have the general interest it does today, and some of the facts gathered were far from accurate and have only been resolved on mature consideration. In spite of searching and enquiry, photographs of several historic events that I witnessed are missing from this book: the Charter Mayor's procession passing our gate in Malden Road, with Mr Marshall waving his feathered hat to me; the opening of the Baths Hall at North Cheam and the splendid concerts held there; the building of St Dunstan's Hill bypass, and seeing King George V and Queen Mary driving along it to the Derby meeting; groping our way to that same road on the night the authorities tried out the blackout, before war came and changed our lives forever.

With the exception of the Nonsuch High School photographs, almost every Cheam picture is my own, found in family albums and scrapbooks, or at antique fairs.

SECTION ONE

The Village

St Dunstan's church, 1905. The present church, its needle spire a landmark for miles around, was built in brick in the year 1864 to the north of the site of two earlier churches. Part of one of these has survived as the Lumley chapel, in which tombs, monuments and smaller memorials from those buildings have been preserved. The cottages and the lych-gate have survived, but part of the ancient wall on the right, once the boundary of West Cheam Manor, was demolished in the erection of the public library. When the church spire is floodlit for special occasions, such as the Queen's coronation in 1953, it is an unforgettable sight.

Whitehall, Malden Road, 1930. Dating from the beginning of the sixteenth century, this is a timber-framed house, associated in its early days with the Fromonde and Lumley families. From 1785 (when the weatherboarding was added) for almost 180 years it was the property of James Killick and his descendants. For a number of years until around 1959 the stables at the rear were occupied by Miss Oldhouse and her horses – Gypsy (who drank tea from a cup), Bandon, Bella, Carol and Trixie – on which local children learned to ride. In modern times the road has been raised, with some loss of the garden wall, and the house has come alive again with guided tours, historical society meetings and other community projects. At its core, however, it remains the house known to Tudor kings and queens.

Two views of Park Lane, 1925. These postcards, published by A. Ainsworth of 26 Malden Road (now 20 The Broadway), show how little change has been allowed over the years to this weatherboarded corner of the old village. Part of the ancient brick wall has been demolished to give access to Elizabeth House.

Laurel Cottage and Vault Cottage, Malden Road, *c. 1925*. These cottages are weatherboarded in the style of neighbouring Whitehall and houses in Park Lane, Ewell Road and elsewhere in Malden Road. A shop-window and name board on one of them is partly obscured by the small central tree. According to tradition there was an undercroft behind this row of cottages. The first pupils of Cheam School are said to have assembled there at the time of the plague of London under the tutelage of George Aldrich of Whitehall. The area was covered in more than sixty years ago.

Members of Cheam Fire Brigade, *c. 1911*. The pump and drier equipment were kept in a building just north of the rectory. All of the firemen were volunteers, carrying on with their normal jobs until an emergency arose. The group's leader, Mr George Bastin (seated left), was also the landlord of The Prince of Wales public house, immediately opposite. By 1929 the small building in Malden Road was being used as a mortuary.

Malden Road, 1904. Looking north today from the entrance to the war memorial gardens one will still find many reminders of this view. The shop (right) was on the corner of Church Road and the frontage of the cottage next door has altered very little in ninety years. Beyond it are the King's Hall ('dances and teas'), a side-road leading to houses that include Honeysuckle Cottage, and The Prince of Wales public house. The Scout Hall (St Dunstan's Institute, left) remains, but an entrance to Mickleham Gardens has been made through the rectory wall. In 1930, when the southern part of Malden Road was renamed The Broadway, the street numbers were adjusted and No. 58, for example, became No. 36.

Pond Hill Cottage, Malden Road, *c.* 1925. It is said that a third storey was added to the original farmhouse at the turn of the century, and the variety of window styles bears this out. The two smaller buildings (right), once part of the farm, were used by Sargeant's (later Express) Dairy. I remember when the electric floats replaced the horse-drawn delivery carts. When the cottage was demolished the present parade of shops was built and Pond Hill Gardens followed. The village pond, which gave its name to the area, was somewhere opposite The Prince of Wales public house.

No. 36 Malden Road, 21 July 1933. The window opening onto the backyard was above the old stone sink in the scullery, and next to that was the brick copper for the weekly washing. This had to be filled with water, which was kept hot by a coal fire beneath. The curtain behind the desk is an attempt at 1930s modesty as it hides the door of the outside (and only) lavatory.

A tight fit on a garden seat, July 1936. The four little girls sitting by the tool shed at 36 Malden Road are, left to right: Rita Owen, Pat Hennessy, Pat Martin, Thelma Earl. Pat Martin lived in Palmer Avenue, and the other three at various Malden Road addresses.

CHEAM
CHARTER FAIR

FRIDAY, 15th MAY, 1953

PROGRAMME

10.45 a.m.	Arrival of Queen of the Fair
10.50 a.m.	,, Canon W. S. Hayman, M.A. RECTOR OF CHEAM
10.55 a.m.	,, Ald. Sir Sidney Marshall, D.L., J.P., M.P. and Miss Marshall Miss Ann Kingsley Williams
11.00 a.m.	Short Service of Dedication led by Canon W. S. Hayman, M.A.
11.10 a.m.	Official Opening Ceremony by Sir Sidney
11.15 a.m.	Crowning of the Queen of the Fair
11.20 a.m.	Official Tour of Inspection

★ ★

6 p.m.	Fancy Dress Competition for Children 6 years to 8 years old
6.30 p.m.	Fancy Dress Competition for Children 9 years to 14 years old
7.30 p.m.	Decorated Cycles assembling at the Century Car Park

**Application for Free Entry for these Competitions should be
made to the official stall on the day of the Fair.**

Charter Fair, coronation year, 1953. For years it was believed that, to keep the right granted in 1259 by King Henry III, a fair must be held every 15 May on the Park Road site. Once, during the Second World War, a man stood alone with a tray of home-made wares so that the privilege should not be forfeited. In 1951, as part of the Festival of Britain, the local Ratepayers' Association revived interest in the event. Since then, although from time to time it is claimed that no charter exists, the fair has become a significant fund-raiser for charity. In my childhood the fair was a modest collection of hoop-la, coconut shies, roll-a-penny and other stalls, where the prize might have been a goldfish, complete with glass bowl.

The coat of arms of the borough of Sutton and Cheam, 1934. The shield is blue with a silver pale on which the four crosses represent the Archbishopric of Canterbury. The keys (red on gold, blue on silver) also appear on the arms of the Benedictine Abbey of Chertsey. Both of these ecclesiastical bodies held lands in the area before the twelfth century. The bird is a popinjay (a parrot with red legs and beak) which also appeared on the arms of the Lumley family. Some featured in the garden statuary of Nonsuch Palace, too, though they were described as 'fawlcons' in a survey carried out in 1650. The words are a quotation from Dr John Hacket, a seventeenth-century rector of Cheam, who maintained his religious principles throughout the Civil War despite imprisonment and death threats. This phrase also appears above the door of the parochial rooms (the parish hall) and on the badge of Nonsuch County School for Girls.

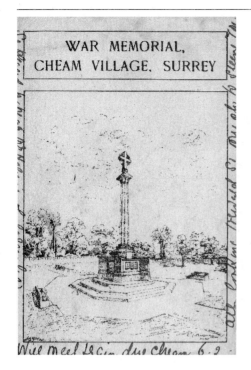

WAR MEMORIAL,
CHEAM VILLAGE. SURREY

The original design for the war memorial, 1920. This postcard drawing is signed by C.J. Marshall, FRIBA, author of *A History of the Old Villages of Cheam and Sutton*, published in 1936. In this book he explains that his design is 'emblematic of sacrifice' and that the carving and installation of the memorial were carried out by Mr Snook of Worcester Park and paid for by public subscription.

The war memorial, 1922. Mr Marshall included the stone benches and field gun to give horizontal lines to balance his design. After a while the gun was removed (I heard that one reason for this was that it turned out to have been an enemy weapon), much to the designer's chagrin. In my childhood there was a magnificent fig tree in the north-west corner of the memorial gardens, overhanging the footpath of Malden Road.

St Dunstan's church, 1911. In 1870 the tower and spire were added to this church, which had been built to Mr T.H. Pownall's design six years earlier. The chancel walls were panelled in 1931, the same year that a new pulpit in memory of Colonel the Hon. Francis Colborne, DL, JP, was given by his widow, Alice, the last private owner of Nonsuch Mansion and estate; that is the interior I remember from Sunday School days. *Travellers Three*, *The Knights of the Holy Grail* and other books signed by successive rectors (Canon H. Wesley Dennis and Canon W.S. Hayman) still stand on my shelves. They are a reminder of my 'exceptional attendance' even in the early days of the Second World War – not so difficult, as my home was only yards away in Malden Road. During the early 1940s the Sunday School was held in a small hall near the Lumley chapel (right).

Love Lane. From Malden Road via the path by the lych-gate, this quiet and secluded path runs from the curve of Church Farm Lane to Gander Green Lane. On the left (north) was Seears Park and meadowland, and on the right the grounds of Mrs Seears's house, The Quarry. Many a Saturday afternoon as a little girl I walked along here with my father, on the way to and from tending my grandfather's grave in Sutton cemetery. There was a squeaking pivoted iron-bar gate to negotiate and the bypass (St Dunstan's Hill) to cross after it was built in the early 1930s. For me, though, a far greater hazard was the sinister low-lying spot known as Boney Hole, where, after periods of heavy rain a bourn occasionally rose through the Thanet sand subsoil of the lane.

Station Road (Malden Road), looking north, *c*. 1890. The curved wall (left) belongs to Mr Boniface's Cheam Brewery, at the junction with the road to Ewell. A map of the village from the mid-nineteenth century shows a right-angled corner to the wall and kerb. After the railway reached Cheam in 1847 it must have become necessary to rebuild the wall in a curve, thus opening up the crossroads. In 1880 the brewery advertised 'Special beers for Harvest 8d per gallon in casks not less than 18 gallons'. The buildings were demolished in 1921 but it is said that the cellars remain beneath today's plots of grass on the same corner. Towards the centre of this view is part of The Old Cottage's roof. It would be another thirty-two years before the building was moved farther along the road. The cottages by the horse and cart also appear on p. 23.

High Street, looking west from Park Road, 1907. This view shows the downhill slope towards the old Harrow Inn, explaining the local tradition that this had so daunted drivers of horse-drawn coaches that they preferred to reach the old London Road via Park Road (far right, with the caution sign).

High Street from Park Road, 1925. This was ten years before the majority of houses were swept away in a road-widening scheme. Not until well into the 1950s was this area fully rebuilt. The milk churn on wheels, covered against the sun, has come from Sargeant's Dairy on Pond Hill.

Malden Road (Station Road), *c.* 1923. At first glance the route 113 general 'scooter' (single-decker bus) is the most notable feature of the past. Closer inspection will reveal (left to right) the original kerb and a surviving tree from Cheam House, the protruding single-storey bakery with its shop behind, White Lodge before the addition of a pitched roof and, behind the bus, old cottages not removed until about 1932, when Mr Sargeant's bicycle shop and the International Stores replaced them.

Malden Road, looking south, *c.* 1928. The shopping centre was redeveloped by the Onyx Property Company in an acceptable mock-Tudor style, possibly reflecting the history of nearby Nonsuch Park. Although the road was not widened into The Broadway until 1930, this part of the village has in almost all other respects remained the same to this day. The Old Cottage, believed to date from the early sixteenth century (as does Whitehall), formerly stood much nearer the crossroads. It was dismantled, refurbished and rebuilt on its present site in 1922, and used as a council rent office for some years.

Malden Road, looking north, *c.* 1928. For more than 150 years Cheam House stood on the far left, originally facing west towards Nonsuch. Its grounds extended from Ewell Road to Park Lane (where the entrance was), and its first owner was John Pybus, whose daughter Kitty married (at St Dunstan's) the poor but witty Revd Sydney Smith, who became the celebrated Canon of St Paul's Cathedral. At some stage the cart-track running behind the house was improved and became Malden Road, and a new entrance was made on this side. After use as a centre for German prisoners of war in the First World War, the house deteriorated and was demolished in 1922.

Crossways Pharmacy, The Broadway, July 1930. The proprietor of the pharmacy has captured his window display and infant customer in this photograph.

The Broadway, 1934. Crossways Pharmacy is the shop with the Kodak pennant. Beyond The Old Cottage, partially hidden by the trees, is the three-storey shop built for Sainsbury's. Older readers will have mixed emotions on being reminded of the open-air steps to the upper deck of the 156 route bus. A Kingston to Belmont 213 'scooter' (formerly the 113 Banstead route) is approaching. (Technical advice from Mr John Bristoll of Eastbourne.)

Cheam Park House, 1938. This house was built in about 1820 for a London tea merchant, Mr A. Palmer, and remained in his family for several generations. The estate extended for a considerable distance north and included the site, given by Mr Palmer in 1826, for the National School for Boys, which was demolished in 1993. Cheam Park's last private owner was Mrs Bethell, and in 1937 it was acquired by Sutton and Cheam Borough Council. The house was severely damaged by a flying bomb in the Second World War and had to be demolished, though the lovely walled garden remained. The rustic bridge was built to provide access across the ha-ha, a boundary ditch.

Cheam Park, 1950. Mrs Bethell allowed the grounds to be used for many fêtes, flower shows and open-air performances. This carried on a tradition begun years before when Sunday School parties came from London to enjoy roundabouts and swings set up at the far end of the park. In June 1953 the coronation of Queen Elizabeth II was celebrated here with a funfair and a 'flower, fur and feather show', including displays of fancy pigeons. The park was the destination of a 5½ mile carnival procession, and the day ended with a pyrotechnic display at dusk, features of which included 'the dance of the tadpoles', a revolving silver fountain and a portrait of Her Majesty in fireworks.

The boating pond, Cheam 'Rec', 1936. It would appear, by the trail of drips and his paddler's footwear, that this boy had just broken the rules and waded in to the pond to retrieve his model yacht. Many a child who frequented the pond brought a long bamboo pole with a cup-hook at one end for the same purpose. On a recent voyage of rediscovery I found the pond still there, though dry. The distant tennis-courts and at least one of the tall trees can also still be identified. My own toy yacht had, most topically, been christened the *Queen Mary* by my two young uncles – the great ocean liner was launched the same year.

The recreation ground, Malden Road. This is a corner of that part of Cheam Park where the funfair for Sunday School parties took place. Celebrations of sovereigns' anniversaries from Queen Victoria to Queen Elizabeth II have been held here too. The June 1953 festivities included a children's tea party, a Boy Scout display and camp, and a youth service attended by the Bishop of Woolwich and Cheam's rector, Canon W.S. Hayman. One can still locate this view, with the path on the right leading to the tennis-courts. One of the three old trees on the left still survives.

The New Smithy, Station Way. For over three hundred years from the end of the sixteenth century the business of ironworkers and farriers was carried on in various smithies in Cheam by the Barnes family. A map of 1867 shows one such building in the yard of the old Harrow Inn, and another in the quarry behind the Railway Hotel. In 1860 Moses Barnes moved across the road from the quarry to this smithy which had been built for him. It was converted into a private residence many years ago.

Station Way, looking south, 1908. The grass and fencing (far left) are part of Moses Barnes's smithy (see above), his earlier building having been some distance behind the bushes (right). A second railway bridge of steel girders was erected alongside this one when the track was widened. The roofs beyond the arch belong to Cold Blow, a house on the corner of Peach's Close. Yet another house believed to incorporate relics of old Nonsuch Palace, it was built for Edward Boniface, the owner of Cheam Brewery.

CENTURY CHEAM VILLAGE

JUNE 28 WEEK

LANZA SINGS AGAIN

MON TUES WED Last show 7 o'c	THURS FRI SAT Last Show

THE TOAST OF NEW ORLEANS

THE GREA CARUSO

TECHNICOLOR 1.45 5.20 8.55 Ⓤ	TECHNICOLOR 1.50 5.15 8.4
LOUIS CALHERN	A FINE PICTURE OF GREAT DA
THE MAN WITH THIRTY SONS	**THE RED BADGE OF COURA**
3.35 7.10 Ⓤ	3.50 7.15

Advertisement for the Century Cinema, Station Way. The cinema was built on the south side of Cheam Court land and opened in 1937. It specialized in rerunning films from earlier years and kept a book in which patrons could enter requests for past favourites. After the Second World War it had a grand reopening with, I believe, James Mason in *The Man in Grey*. It finally closed in 1960. The foyer was demolished to make way for a petrol station and the auditorium was converted into an office block. Thirty years later the site was completely developed, but it happily retains the Century name.

Cheam station, looking east, c. 1920. This view is from the end of the Up platform towards the steel Hale's Bridge, introduced in 1909 when the station was redeveloped with a better fast service to London. Additional tracks and sidings were laid, and the two subway skylights show where it was intended to have a central platform for use with express trains.

Cheam station, looking west, 1920. How the grand scheme came to naught (partly because of the First World War) can be better appreciated in this view from the bridge, which was superceded by a wide concrete structure when the bypass was built, in about 1928.

Footpath and signal-box, Cheam station. This signal-box was built at the west end of the Up platform in 1911 and served the station for nearly seventy years, its structure being little altered. Immediately below the wooden steps are the side walls of the brick railway arch, and Moses Barnes's smithy is to the left on the far side of Station Way (see p. 29). This footpath ran for more than a quarter of a mile between the line and the back gardens of Anne Boleyn's Walk, emerging in Ewell Road by Harefield Bridge.

St Mary's Children's Home opening, 58 Sandy Lane, 6 November 1914. Chesham Close was developed on the site some time after the home closed in 1968. Any details or reminiscences would be welcomed.

St Mary's home. The 'orphanage girls' I remember attending St Dunstan's Sunday School may have come from here.

The tennis-courts, Meadowside Road, 1935. Situated on the corner of Sandy Lane, today the courts form part of the Cheam Fields Club. The pavilion, though considerably altered, has survived. This postcard was produced by D.G. Rix of Malden Road, Cheam. His premises still exist (between the Baptist church and the war memorial gardens), though in a 1929 street directory they are listed as Cheam post office, and in one of 1938 as a mail order office.

No. 63 Sandy Lane, 1933. This house was built in 1928 and survives in its now mature garden setting, with some alterations and additions, among neighbouring houses of markedly different design.

The Brownie pack, St Andrew's Presbyterian church, Northey Avenue, 1951. The pack, which met weekly in the church hall, was led at this time by Tawny Owl Pat Hennessy. This photograph was taken by senior helper Greta Hughes. From December 1927 the hall, built along traditional lines on a site purchased three years earlier, was used for worship. The church, designed in contemporary style, was dedicated on 8 July 1933.

Cheam Girl Guides, 1950s. Divisional Commissioner Miss Muriel Firth gives the Guide handshake to company leader Janet Browne, watched by patrol leader Valerie Thompson. She is presenting them with their Queen's Guide badges and certificates.

Cheam Road, looking east. This William Pile postcard, sent in 1907 by 'MW' from Oakleigh, Sutton, shows the old narrow road once barred by a toll-gate. The barrier was moved from the Cock Hotel crossroads at Sutton in about 1837 as the town developed westwards. On the left is Gander Green Lane, with York Road opposite. For a number of years from the mid-1950s we called the house built on the site of the toll-house 'Secombe Corner', since the well-known singer and comedian, now Sir Harry, lived there with his family. Carlton House and Wrighton Court have since replaced his home on the west corner of York Road.

Cheam Road, looking west from Sutton, 1907. The right-hand turning is Sherwood Park Road. Sutton High School (below) is almost opposite.

Sutton High School, 1907. This girls' school is almost opposite the entrance to Sherwood Park Road (above). Three thousand past and present pupils of the school celebrated its centenary in St Paul's Cathedral in March 1984.

Robin Hood Lane. In places the old road from Cheam to Sutton has changed beyond recognition. The discovery of this 1908 postcard served as a shock reminder of the time, not so long ago, when the tree-lined south end of Robin Hood Lane gave directly onto the main road. 'In the summer the road is lovely', wrote the sender. The twin-gabled inn, named after the lane, came into view at the foot of the hill as one turned the corner from Cheam. The inn still survives.

Mulgrave Road, 1903. Running parallel with the A232 Cheam road, the prosperously residential Mulgrave Road was once a quieter and safer alternative route for a cyclist from Sutton railway station. The original lane ran west for only half a mile. A slight left-hand curve indicates where it was extended at the turn of the century to run past Cheam station and connect with Sandy Lane.

SECTION TWO
Nonsuch Park

The Mansion, Nonsuch Park, 1950s. Not to be confused with Henry VIII's palace, built half a mile to the south-east over 250 years before, this house was designed by Jeffry Wyatt in 1802 for Mr Samuel Farmer. Wyatt went on to reconstruct Windsor Castle (for which he was knighted) using similar medieval and 'fairy tale' ideas tried out at Nonsuch Park. The trees and bushes (right) are growing in the Dell, a turfed-over chalk-pit, which may have been dug to provide building materials for the Tudor palace. At the beginning of 1959 a clock was installed on the mansion, commemorating the 21st anniversary of the park being acquired by the neighbouring local authorities of Sutton and Cheam, and Epsom and Ewell, for public enjoyment.

ROSE WALK. NONSUCH PARK. CHEAM.

Rose Walk, Nonsuch Park House. The first house on the mansion site was erected for Joseph Thompson in about 1731 and survives today, incorporated into the nineteenth-century building. His descendant Thomas Whately wrote a famous book, *Observations on Modern Gardening*, two hundred years later. The grounds still reflect this special interest. Arbours, pergolas, ancient walls, stone seats in sunny corners, a sundial, and a water-lily pond with a fountain are features I remember from visits to the park. A tradition of growing lilacs is said to have arisen from the first 'lelack trees' in England having been brought to Nonsuch Park.

The Chestnut Walk, 1930s. Some of these beautiful trees still stand sixty years on, but the park railings have not survived and the laurel bushes (left) have made way for the approach to the car park. It is gratifying to see how much enjoyment is derived nowadays from this open space, dedicated in 1937 to the people of Sutton and Cheam, Epsom and Ewell. The 263 acres then cost more than £100,000.

Bell Gate and Lodge, Nonsuch Park, 1930s. Beyond the gates lies Ewell Road, which leads to Cheam village. The lodge was demolished in 1938, at about the same time that Nonsuch County School for Girls was being built nearby. These gates became the rear (pupils') entrance to the school. On the other side of the park Redgate Lodge on London Road, Ewell, survived until 1955.

Bell Gate and memorial, Ewell Road, 1912. The fountain was erected by the sons and daughters of Mr Farmer of Nonsuch Park, 'to the glory of God and the memory of those gone before'. The postbox and iron side gate have not survived, and the dedication carved on the monument is now partially worn away. For over fifty-five years the girls of Nonsuch have passed through this gate *en route* to the rear entrance to the grounds.

Park Cottages, Ewell Road, *c.* 1935. The middle cottage (front door partly hidden by bush) was my home in the 1950s, and the interior retained many quaint features from earlier days. The doorways were low and wide with sills worn wafer-thin, and a lift-the-latch door opened directly onto the foot of the steep, boxed-in stairway. Standing opposite the Bellgate entrance to Nonsuch Park, and weatherboarded like those in Park Lane, Malden Road and Park Road, the cottages were probably built for palace estate workers.

The men who built Nonsuch, 1937–8. In 1914 land in Sutton was assigned for a new girls' school for the borough, but it was later acquired by the Southern Railway. Another site at the south-east corner of Nonsuch Park was chosen, and the ceremonial cutting of the first sod occurred at 11.30 a.m. on Wednesday 30 December 1936, by the Mayor Alderman Sidney Marshall, supported by Alderman J. Chuter Ede, MP, Chairman of Surrey County Council. The architects were Messrs Jarvis and Richards.

The art room, 1938. Among photographs of schoolrooms prior to occupation on 3 May is this one featuring the more easterly of the two third-floor practical rooms. The other room was for domestic science and was fitted with cookers, work tables, sinks and so on. In the school's early days the front staircase was generally out of bounds to pupils and yet gave the only access to the top floor. Going to classes in one of these two rooms therefore held a touch of adventure.

Surrey County Council.

Nonsuch County School for Girls.

The Chairman and the Governors
request the honour of the company of

J. A. Parker, Esq, _____ *and Lady*

at the Official Opening of the School

by The Right Honourable Earl Stanhope,
K.G. D.S.O. M.C. D.L.
(President of the Board of Education)

on Monday, 20th June, 1938, at 3 p.m.
(Guests are asked to be seated by 2.45 p.m. at the latest).

R.S.V.P. TO THE HEADMISTRESS OF THE SCHOOL NOT LATER THAN 30TH MAY, 1938, ON RECEIPT OF YOUR ACCEPTANCE AN ADMISSION TICKET WILL BE ISSUED.

Invitation to the official opening of Nonsuch. Miss Dickie, nine members of staff and 180 girls assembled on the first day of school on 3 May 1938. It was raining heavily. Seven weeks later (20 June) the official ceremony took place, with much comment on the twenty-five year delay in building the school. Nonsuch was originally intended to accommodate 490 pupils but only gradually built up to that number. It was 1941 before there were enough girls of the right age to make up a sixth form.

Miss M.M. Dickie, MA. Marion McConnell Dickie became the first headmistress of Nonsuch at the age of thirty-seven. The new school had been open for precisely a year and four months when the Second World War broke out. Over the next six years Miss Dickie shouldered many additional responsibilities, some of which have come to light only in the research for this book. Among the large-scale problems were shortages and rationing of food, clothing, petrol and fuel; air raids (how to get hundreds of girls speedily into the shelters to carry on lessons, or even sit school certificate examinations); the blackout; evacuation; fire-watching; one-parent families (while fathers were away in the forces); and unexploded bombs in the school grounds. Miss Dickie retired in 1964, but seventeen years later resumed her central place in the school hall for an evening when over three hundred former pupils and staff gathered to celebrate her eightieth birthday. Her birth in 1901 qualified her as a Victorian, as she was proud to remind us. She died in August 1985, and a memorial service was held at St Andrew's Presbyterian church, Northey Avenue.

Opposite, bottom: Guests of honour at the official opening ceremony. Those present include Mr Horace Sharp, Commander Sir Archibald Southby MP, Countess Stanhope, the Earl of Stanhope (president of the Board of Education), Sir Philip Henriques (chairman of Surrey County Council) and Alderman J. Chuter Ede MP. A silver bowl of roses was presented to Countess Stanhope to mark the occasion.

Nonsuch games officials, 1954–5. This is a rare photograph showing the early winter uniform. Standing, left to right: Judith Champion, Susan Lacey, Margaret Lodde, Susan Beatty, Vivienne Smith. Seated: Ruth Raeburn, Ann Denner, Dolores Cohen. Worn with a light-blue blouse and (originally) plain tie, the navy pinafore dress with a V-neck and flared skirt, when introduced in 1938, was a far cry from the traditional box-pleated gymslip.

The staff with Miss Dickie, 1946–7. Those present by the square pool in the quadrangle include Miss E.M. Bessey, Miss Boshier, Miss M.A. Cavenagh, Mrs C.M. Darroch, Miss K.M. Dormer, Miss Evans (Mrs Howell), Miss M. Farrant, Miss S. Faust, Miss R. Finlay, Miss F.E. Hemming, Miss Jewsbury, Miss Leopold, Miss K.M. Nicholls, Miss G. Rowlands, Miss H.M. Sharpe, Miss M. Taylor, Miss M. Varley, Mrs J. Wells, Mrs Wheeler and Miss K.M. Woods.

Opposite, bottom: *Alice in Wonderland*, Nonsuch, 14/15 December 1945. The players included Barbara Pearce, Edna Squires, Janet Cox, Hilda Byles, Pamela Clark, Anita Harvey, Joyce Templeman and Jean Harling. The play was adapted from Lewis Carroll's story and produced by Mrs C.M. Darroch (Miss Holman) in aid of the careers fund, piano fund, Dramatic Society and assorted school charities. During the croquet scene Hilda had to remove the Dodo head to play her own incidental music at the piano. After weeks of messy work in the art room with shredded newspaper and flour-and-water paste (not easy to find in the last days of wartime), Miss Varley and her sixth form helpers produced the characters' heads and masks.

The Tempest, 14 December 1946. Nonsuch girls in this scene include Hazel Benson (Prospero), Brenda Gardner (Ferdinand) and Jennifer Keast (Miranda). Produced by Mrs C.M. Darroch, the play was put on in aid of the careers fund. The scenery was made by Miss Varley and helpers. The lighting and effects were managed by my old classmates Jeannine ('Ninette') Ash and Anita ('Ann') Harvey.

The Tempest, 14 December 1946. Another charming scene from the play shows Ariel, played by Joyce Luff, with Hazel Benson as Prospero.

Outside the staff room, summer 1945. Miss Rosemary Finlay (left) was the school's music teacher. She trained and conducted the choirs, including those that sang for *The Tempest*. Miss Sylvia Faust (right) was our piano teacher, and she accompanied dancing lessons and singing. She composed most of the *Alice in Wonderland* music and performed Chopin brilliantly.

The sixth form in the quadrangle, summer 1947. Among the girls in this group are Jeannine Ash, Olive Bottle, Hilda Byles, Celia Cockshutt, Josephine Cottrell, Barbara Hollis, Cecily McDaniel, Margaret Monk, Valerie Neil, Constance Sibley, Edna Squires, Joyce Templeman, Sheila Thorpe and Rosemary Wells.

The Mikado, 1948. Pamela Utting is the Mikado (elevated, right). Those in the front row include Sheila Davis (far left, wielding the fan) and Christine Land (third from left, with dark obi).

Speech Day, 21 July 1950. Among the distinguished guests on the platform, listening to the address by the headmistress, Miss Dickie, are the Rector of Cheam, Canon W.S. Hayman, Mrs Rosemary Hayman and Alderman Mrs Daisy Sparks, who was the Mayor of Sutton and Cheam during the twenty-first anniversary celebrations of the granting of the borough's charter.

Nonsuch tennis team, 1966–7. Standing, left to right: Gillian Perrin, Ruth Scott, Susan Robinson, Jackie Bedford. Seated: Pat Parkin, Diana Doorley. Gillian progressed via table tennis (from the age of eight) and tennis to badminton championship standard, where she is better known internationally by her married name of Gillian Gilks.

Speech Day, 17 July 1953. The singing is being conducted by Mrs R.W. Probert. By tradition the names of head girls and girls gaining university places were recorded on the panelling of the hall, beginning with Myfanwy Rowlands in 1942. Part of the list is visible behind the heads of the singers. Through the window is a view across the playground towards the trees that form the boundary with Nonsuch Park.

The Rivals, December 1951. Breeches roles abound when an all-girls' school tackles a play with almost a dozen male characters. Among Nonsuch pupils following the 'travesty' tradition of Mrs Bracegirdle, Nell Gwynne, Madame Vestris and Sarah Bernhardt were Valerie Downton, Christine Hickox, Antonia Raeburn, Jessie Havers, Angela Jeffreys, Brenda Howell, Maureen Taylor, Beryl Horsnell, Dorothy Stone, Audrey Hodgins and Eileen Gurr.

Nonsuch tennis team, 1960–1. Standing, left to right: Sally Speer, Phillipa Dore-Smith, Mary Rodhouse, Cheryl Shepheard. Seated: Mary Shannon, Diana Hicks. Mary Shannon was a champion table tennis player.

North Cheam

The Queen Victoria, North Cheam crossroads. This old inn, built where the London Road toll-gate once stood, was replaced in 1936 by an impressive roadhouse with a large forecourt. Less than thirty years later the area was redeveloped and the third inn is now sited less conspicuously. Nalder and Collyer's 'Entire', as announced on the old façade, applies to a mixture of beer and two kinds of ale known as porter. Being mixed together in the barrel and not in the tankard, it was served up 'entire'.

The Crossroads. One of the oldest junctions in the area, until a century ago this was the site on Cheam Common of a toll-gate on the London to Epsom road. The lane that led to the south became Malden Road. The shopping area was redeveloped in the mid-1930s with wide pavements, flower-beds and modern architecture. The Granada cinema opened in 1937. My father with the Joint Electricity Authority (p. 109) helped to install the giant central 'lampshade' in the auditorium, and there were Saturday morning Granadiers children's shows. Does anyone reading this remember singing 'Granada, Granada, London Road, North Cheam' to the tune of 'Funiculi, funicula', or taking part in the talent contests?

Stonecot Hill. A few yards beyond St Anthony's Hospital this short stretch of the A24 London road lies between Ridge Road and Sutton Common Road (p. 81) on the south. The central shop, Martell's, at Nos 10–14, was advertised in 1966 as 'the complete house furnishers'. It also ran a storage and removals office opposite Sutton railway station at Blandford House, 2 Mulgrave Road, adjacent to the *Sutton and Cheam Advertiser* offices. The company promised 'courteous and efficient service at a reasonable cost'.

C.T. Brock & Company, pyrotechnic manufacturers. From 1901 'Brock's Crystal Palace Fireworks' were made under scrupulously regulated conditions at their premises off Gander Green Lane. For over thirty years Roman candles, rockets, golden rain, giant firecrackers and Catherine wheels were produced in small buildings widely dispersed over many acres of old Cheam Common. This area was later developed as the Brock's estate, with roads bearing the names of towns on the River Thames. White overalls denoted workers packing and despatching fireworks to worldwide destinations, while those who handled the explosive powder wore black.

St Anthony's Convent and Hospital, London Road. Sœur Marie Thérèse founded the Daughters of the Cross on 8 September 1833. Their early work was among poor children and women prisoners. After fifteen years they established a training hospital in Dusseldorf, then in 1904 moved to North Cheam House, London Road, formerly The Lord Nelson coaching inn. They transformed the billiard room into their oratory and worshipped there until their purpose-built hospital was opened.

St Anthony's Hospital. Designed by James Emes and built by J. Tapley Limited, the new hospital opened at the beginning of the First World War and was soon asked to take in sick and wounded soldiers. These patients found themselves being nursed in a hospital with many of the latest features, including a Waygood-Otis lift between floors. During Sutton and Cheam's 1934 charter celebrations, which coincided with the hospital's 30th anniversary, the mayor's procession paused for commemorative group photographs on the front steps of the hospital.

A pavilion in the grounds of St Anthony's Hospital. From 1907 various pavilions were built to accommodate patients who might benefit from open-air nursing. These developed into a sanatorium, which continued to take children until 1934. A cemetery for members of the Order occupied another part of the grounds, and between 1907 and 1966 more than a hundred sisters were buried there. When the new hospital complex was completed the cemetery was transformed into a tranquil garden of remembrance.

Steve Donoghue. The staff and supporters of St Anthony's Hospital have, throughout its history, applied themselves to fund-raising. Their summer fêtes, attended by celebrities and former patients, are warmly remembered more than fifty years on. It was in 1933 that the people's favourite celebrity, champion jockey Steve Donoghue, rode the winner of the donkey derby.

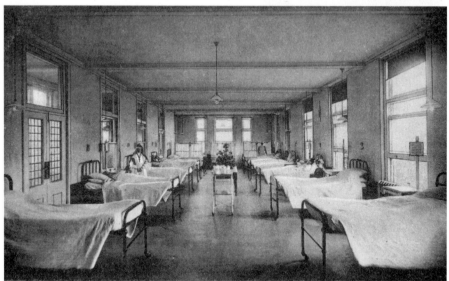

St Teresa's Ward, St Anthony's Hospital. An additional wing had to be built on to the new hospital only eight years after it opened. After the Second World War yet more room was made by enclosing the balconies that for so long had contributed to the fresh-air cures encouraged by the hospital. On 3 September 1973 Sister Mary Perpetua cut the first turf for the building (by John Laing Construction Limited) of a new hospital, which received its first patient twenty-one months later.

Worcester Park

The station. The line was cut in 1859 by the London and South Western Railway (the livery of which was salmon pink and brown) to link Epsom and Waterloo via Wimbledon. As mansions were built on the former Nonsuch Great Park (Worcester Park) the line served a developing commuter area. City businessmen were driven to the station in their carriages. The writer H.G. Wells lived here for a time. Polo and hunting helped to fill the leisure hours of the new residents. The railway line was electrified in the mid-1920s.

Cheam Common Road, 1905. Beneath much of the built-up area from the present Worcester Park to St Dunstan's church in Cheam lies old Cheam Common. The most northerly part formed the pre-1933 boundary with the parish of Cuddington. Tradition has it that, during the seventeenth-century civil war, royalists and parliamentarians skirmished in this area. Building and redevelopment over the past ninety years have left few landmarks to help identify features of the old common in these postcards.

The Plough Inn, Manor Drive. This inn, on the southern corner of Malden Road, is readily identifiable. We senior schoolgirls in 1944–5 had the opportunity to do our bit for the war effort by helping on a farm to the west of this area.

Manor Drive. This view and that above feature on postcards from a series produced some forty years ago and illustrate how some areas survive little changed. These houses, at the junction with Highdown, are easily recognized.

Worcester Park House, 1922. This was said to be the house built in about 1800 by William Taylor junior, son of the owner of the powder mill on the banks of the Hogsmill river (p. 74). When the mill blew up, one night in 1742, residents for miles around assumed that the great explosion was an earthquake.

Old Malden Lane, 1905. Pleasantly leafy and rural as of old (if heavy traffic can be disregarded), this lane has an attractive inn at its south end named after the Hogsmill river. Barrow Hill beyond is a reminder of Saxon settlements and burial grounds in this part of the county. At this point the river, on its way north to join the Thames at Kingston, the Greater London/Surrey boundary and Old Malden Lane run in parallel.

SECTION FIVE

Ewell

No. 32 High Street. For generations the Williams family, sometimes in partnership as Brunton and Williams, has occupied the stationers and bookshop opposite The King William IV Inn (formerly The George and Dragon). The name, windows and low-ceilinged interior have changed little since, but the range of goods sold today is much wider.

The centre of the village of Ewell, looking north towards the Horse Pond and Spring Corner (among the trees). The access to that part of the High Street was created in 1834 by removing 'the town house' referred to in Tudor times. The Market House (far right) is thought to be nearly four hundred years old, and the cottages (Nos 11, 13 and 15) with jettied upper storeys date from some fifty years earlier.

The centre of Ewell village, looking south. Church Street is on the left and The King William IV Inn is in the centre. Over a ten-year period archaeological digs at the rear of the inn yielded many Roman artefacts. Close inspection of the High Street façade of the house on the corner of West Street (far right) will reveal that it is not made of solid brick but hung with 'mathematical' tiles, which give that illusion. The application of these tiles is explained clearly in a display at Bourne Hall Museum.

The Horse Pond and dipping place. Until 1834, when a turnpike road was made to connect the north end of the High Street with the old London road, stepping stones were the only way to ford the water here. The pond gave a welcome cooling not only to the hooves of draught horses and cattle being brought to market, but to their drivers and the wheels of the carts. Animals from the occasional travelling circus have also been pictured wading in the water. I remember it as a good place to fish for newts and tadpoles.

Bourne Hall School for Girls. This house, formerly known as Garbrand Hall, was situated on land cleared of farm cottages in about 1770. It was the country seat for a succession of prosperous families and by 1879 was famed for its gardens, especially the azaleas. In the mid-1920s it became a girls' school. This view featured in a 1952 advertisement when the headmistress was Miss M.A. Palmer, BA. The fees were quoted as 'Boarders from 35 gns, day pupils from 12 gns, kindergarten from 7 gns'. The school closed unexpectedly the following year.

The lake (above) and the Dutch Garden (below), Bourne Hall. The formal gardens, ornamental lake and Ionic temple were all relics of a more leisured age. After the girls' school closed the hall stood empty while its future was debated. It was finally demolished in 1962 and the present Bourne Hall community centre, with local museum, public library and exhibition halls, was erected some eight years later. Though the fashion in gardens has changed, the modern setting is very pleasant and peaceful.

Spring Corner, looking north and south, 1920s. The attractively weatherboarded Spring Hotel was once a farmhouse, facing Bourne Hall to the west and Glyn House (formerly Rectory House) to the east. Until 1834, when this stretch of road was created, the Hogsmill river had to be forded at this point, and access to the main roads to London and Kingston was via the dog-leg of Church Street. The Venture coach-and-four (below) made a number of promotional journeys from London to Brighton, as well as to Epsom race meetings.

Going to the races, London Road, *c.* 1920. One mounted policeman is in control of this traffic jam passing the Spring Hotel (far left). The garden wall (right) belongs to the Glyn family home, Rectory House. The bus drivers are wearing their white coats and the trees are in full leaf, so this may be a Derby Day crowd, though they are warmly clad. 'Let's go to Lyons' advertised on the side of the leading omnibus refers to the popular tearooms and Corner House restaurants.

The old parish church and tower. The nave of the old church of St Mary the Virgin dated from the thirteenth century, and there may have been even earlier remains. A gallery was added at the beginning of the nineteenth century, increasing the seating capacity by more than a third, but still the building was deemed inadequate and beyond repair. In 1847 it was demolished, the bells, altar, chancel screen, Tudor pulpit and many ancient memorials being preserved for the new church. The fifteenth-century tower (below) remains to this day. It was for a time used as a mortuary and is now registered as an ancient monument.

St Mary's parish church, 1913. The present church was built in fourteen months and was consecrated in the summer of 1848. Several of the gravestones (to the right of the path, above) are in memory of members of the Williams family (p. 63) and span more than two centuries. Inside (below) the 1897 pulpit of alabaster and marble with vivid green pillars is featured on a postcard published by the Williams's High Street shop. This part of the church escaped a fire in 1973. The north aisle, lady chapel and organ, all of which suffered major damage, were rebuilt within two years of the disaster.

The Green Man Inn, High Street, 1950s. The name of this inn is similar to The Woodman at Ashtead, as foresters sometimes dressed in green. The bus stop served the Nos 406, 408 and 470 routes. It has since been resited farther to the south, beyond the entrance to Reigate Road.

Green Man Street (now the High Street), 1900. This part of the street is believed to run very close to the ancient Fair Field and the route of the Roman road of Stane Street. Ewell formerly held a weekly market and two annual fairs. Only the building bearing Mr Dunford's advertisement can be readily identified ninety years on. The cottages and The Lord Nelson Inn (left) were demolished for road widening, and the Congregational church, whose spire dominates the centre of this view, was removed in 1938 when a larger church was built in London Road. A small memorial garden now occupies the site.

Ewell Castle, from the park, 1904. In the reign of King Charles I an earlier castle stood here. Nearby Ox Lane was the scene of a civil war skirmish in 1648. One of the last owners before the castle was rebuilt in 1814 was Thomas Calverley. The Gadesden family occupied the present building for almost a century. The site of the banqueting hall of Nonsuch Palace was in the castle grounds until the sweep of parkland was riven in the mid-1930s by the bypass road.

The Mill Pond. In a village whose very name suggests the presence of water, this pool has been one of the largest and most picturesque. The nearby spring from which the Hogsmill river rises has been claimed as one of the coldest in the country. Flour, paper and gunpowder are among the goods produced by Ewell's two ancient mills. The Domesday entry for Ewell (1086) includes 'II molini' (two mills).

Across the Hogsmill river, 1907. The brick pack-horse bridge crosses the Hogsmill river on Ewell Court land. The original bridge is believed to date from the eighteenth century, but it has been restored more than once. Several other footbridges allow pleasant walks through The Wilderness on both banks of this modest river. Only in modern times has Ruxley Lane (named after Rokesley, a fifteenth-century owner of the land) been built over the water, replacing the spectacular ford known locally as the 'splash'.

Court Farm Road. Ewell Court House was completed in 1879 for J.H. Bridges of the gunpowder mills, of which nothing now remains but gravestones in St Mary's churchyard that commemorate the victims of explosions. The farmhouse nearby, remembered in the name of this road, was demolished some sixty years ago.

Reigate Road. In 1911 a new arrival in the area sent this postcard from Lynwood, The Green, Ewell Downs Road. Because so little is recognizable today, I quote from her message: 'Ewell Downs Road is a turning off at the top of this hill. We are 25 minutes from the station and shops.' A few of the beautiful horse chestnut trees may have survived.

Two approaches to Stoneleigh station. The station opened in 1932 on the Waterloo to Epsom line. On Kingston Road (above) in 1938 the sign is of interest (right): 'Southern Electric . . . frequent trains – cheap fares'. Items of street furniture to compare include the swan-necked lamp standard and the concrete telephone kiosk beside it. The Broadway (below), with Dell Road and Woodside Avenue to the left and right of the central island, is the south-eastern approach to the station.

Timbercroft, Kingston Road. This road lies in one of the attractively developed areas to the north of the main road, where the old Ewell Common adjoined Nonsuch Great Park. Properties at the Kingston Road end of Timbercroft were destroyed by enemy flying bombs in the Second World War.

A springtime study. This fine picture is endorsed 'Easter 1926' and bears the address Rossmore, Heatherside Road, West Ewell. Perhaps the happy group had walked down the woodland path towards the Hogsmill river.

All Saints' church, West Ewell. Built in 1893 as a daughter church of St Mary's (p. 70). All Saints' did not become independent for almost sixty years. The growth of trees and development of houses beside the footpath (above) leading away from the Hogsmill river renders this view hard to recognize today. The eastern aspect of All Saints' from Church Road (below) has altered little, but the south aisle and community centre (rear) were added in the 1970s.

Cuddington church.

Cuddington bowling green. A housing development on Sparrow Farm land has perpetuated the name of the ancient village, which was laid waste for the creation of King Henry VIII's parks. The Beverley brook runs north to south through the recreation ground.

Gymnastics at Ruxley Lane School.
Barry Dinsdale makes a spectacular leap
under the supervision of Mr Victor
Blore.

The dining-room, Chessington Zoo, 1940s. Little more than four miles from either
Cheam or Belmont, the zoological gardens, circus and funfair have for many years been
a favourite day out for local children. The house, known as Burnt Stub, is all that
remains of a much larger manor, Chessington Hall, where the novelist Fanny Burney
often stayed. The pleasure grounds have now been updated and go by the title of 'The
World of Adventures'.

Sutton Common Road (above) and Gander Green Lane (below). These roads run on parallel courses east to west, linking Sutton with the A24 London road at North Cheam. Past owners of East Cheam Manor, one of the estates bordering Gander Green Lane, included the Lumley, Fromond, Antrobus and Tate families, all of which are remembered in modern road names.

The South Metropolitan District Schools.

Belmont

Belmont's brief history could not be a much greater contrast to Cheam's ancient chronicles, yet the two villages are neighbours, little more than a mile apart. While Cheam grew prosperous under Queen Elizabeth I's patronage, the stark downland to the south saw only a few visitors who came for a day's hunting or racing, and supported a small number of farm workers, shepherds, smallholders and chalk-pit workers.

When a map of Surrey was produced in 1762 the chief feature on this part of Banstead Downs was a semi-basement inn of ill repute known as Little Hell. Anyone travelling the lonely Brighton road risked encounters with highwaymen, footpads, rustlers and the like, and the inn may have been the rogues' meeting-place. That some of them were brought to justice is suggested by the discovery some years ago of a possible gibbet site near Banstead crossroads.

One act of lawlessness was indirectly responsible for the early development of Belmont. In 1849 John Gibbons, the grandson of the proprietor of Little Hell, absconded to America rather than face a charge of poaching. He joined the rush of prospectors to the newly found gold mines of California. Not for him the back-break of digging for gold; he opened a store where he sold provisions, and tools with which others worked. He made his fortune and came home, in time to take advantage of the changes that were planned for the area.

Social consciences were beginning to stir throughout the nation at this time, two aspects of which were to have a lasting influence here. The streets of London were scattered with lost, homeless and delinquent children 'likely to fall under the evil influences of crime, drunken-ness and prostitution'. For some of them the South Metropolitan District School was set up in 1852 on a site overlooking the

Brighton road. Within a few years the school became so overcrowded that a further section had to be built. Twenty years later, on Hundred Acre Farm at the Carshalton end of the Downs, the Middlesex county authorities built their third 'lunatic asylum', housing 2,500 mental patients.

These two vast enterprises generated considerable traffic in passengers, building materials and supplies. 'California' station on the London, Brighton & South Coast Railway line to Epsom Downs opened in May 1865. That exotic title, a colourful reminder of John Gibbons's colourful past, was changed after missing items for the new asylum were traced to the dockside, misdirected and about to make a transatlantic crossing. 'Belmont' seems a poor substitute, especially to those, like myself, who were born there, but the choice could have been something even less imaginative.

Once established the village grew quickly, most of the early inhabitants being employees of the big institutions and their families. Belmont has now become a community in its own right, and the schools and hospitals have changed beyond recognition. A local newspaper recently described Belmont as 'one of the most sought-after residential areas', yet the heart of the village, as commemorated in this book, has changed very little. If they returned today, Sir Sidney Marshall, Mr and Mrs Tertis, the Revd and Mrs Wheeler, and the many other residents who knew the place so long ago would soon feel at home again.

Photography and Belmont are of much the same age, so it has been possible to chart the village's progress with some ease. On the debit side the lack of old buildings and other historic features limited the choice of subjects for the camera in the early days. It has been quite hard to find studies of locations other than the station, the schools, the hospitals, Station Road and Rex's corner!

I spent my teenage years (roughly corresponding to the Second World War and the consequent austerity era) at various addresses in Belmont. I have developed a belated affection for my birthplace, which has prompted me in my later exile in Sussex to collect pictures to remind me of the area.

More than the upheavals that occurred in the war years, and more than the contrast between life in suburban Cheam and downside Belmont, one noticed other changes. Seldom did the Kleeneze man with his suitcase of brushes come to the door, or the gypsy with her wooden clothes-pegs and artificial flowers, or the turbaned Indian pedlar selling scent. Commercial travellers no longer arrived by cab to display the latest range of goods to the shopkeepers, or called on housewives with samples of merchandise, hoping to win their custom.

The strangers in our streets were members of the forces stationed nearby, or on leave, and enemy prisoners of war worked on our farms. Local hospital places were taken up by the 'blue boys' – sick and wounded servicemen wearing ill-fitting royal blue suits, though retaining their regimental headgear. Many other people were in uniform: Land Army girls, air raid wardens and helpers, auxiliary police, firemen, nurses, and members of the Home Guard and the Women's Voluntary Service abounded. Adults ran forces' canteens, collected National Savings, acted as fire watchers and air raid shelter marshals, and women worked in factories and shops to free men for active service. 'Comforts for the troops' – sea-boot stockings, mittens, scarves, balaclava helmets – were knitted in navy, khaki and air force blue.

Even Boy Scouts, Girl Guides and other youth organizations were encouraged to appear in uniform whenever possible. We acted as messengers, joined salvage drives for waste paper and tin foil, worked our own vegetable patches 'digging for victory', and helped to raise money for the Spitfire Fund, Warships Week and other campaigns. Unfortunately, few of these dramatic events are included here, as photographic film was seldom available to the general public. Like many other commodities taken for granted in the 1930s, they were channelled almost exclusively into the war effort. It was twenty years before such items began to return to our shops.

Rediscovered acquaintances have helped with photographs covering the last seventy years, and the albums and reminiscences of older friends and relations have been mercilessly raided to fill the gaps in a village record that has so far received scant attention from local historians. In particular my mother's memories, stretching back some eighty-five years to her childhood in Belmont (and even earlier in Banstead), have been invaluable. Now that the book is finished she, as much as I, can take a breather.

Station Road, looking towards the railway bridge, 1950s. Once post-war austerities were gone, the twenty or so shops in the village were able to cater for most needs. There were also cafés, hairdressers, barbers, petrol stations, doctors and veterinary surgeries, the post office, and a bank on the corner of Belmont Road. Although the shop buildings have changed little in some forty years, closer inspection will reveal great differences in the commodities available today.

The Village

Old Tollgate, Brighton Road (from a Victorian print). The last siting of this toll-gate is said to have been near Sutton Lodge, though until the mid-nineteenth century it had stood at Sutton crossroads. The bar was moved south to keep pace with the gradual spread of residential development. The system was abolished in 1882 and the old bars and toll-houses were removed.

Belmont railway station, *c.* 1906. The London, Brighton & South Coast Railway extended the 1839 London Bridge to Sutton line twenty-six years later, passing farther south through Banstead and terminating at Epsom Downs. The name 'Belmont' was adopted in October 1875 after the original title, 'California', led to errors in goods deliveries. It is said that builders, waiting in vain for the arrival of materials for the construction of Banstead Hospital, ran them to earth on the dockside from where they were about to be shipped across the Atlantic. In 1906 the stationmaster was Mr Hayward Knight.

Banstead Mental Hospital (the 'Asylum'). The hospital (3rd Middlesex County Lunatic Asylum) was built on Hundred Acre Farm on the edge of the downs at Belmont. The extent of the farm, sometimes known as Mount Pleasant (with a windmill), had remained the same since Tudor times. The hospital was built to accommodate 2,500 patients and opened on 23 March 1877, with Mr T. Claye Shaw as medical superintendent.

Banstead Mental Hospital laundry staff, c. 1885. New faces appeared in Belmont as men working on the hospital, together with nurses, attendants and domestic staff, set up home. Cottages were built in Downs Road and elsewhere, and the first shops were opened. Part of this photograph, which included my grandfather and aunt, was too badly cracked to be reproduced here. The hospital closed in 1987.

Downs Road, looking east from Brighton Road, 1900. Behind the cottage and outhouses (left) was a chalk-pit with kilns, and homes for the pit workers. The pit was probably that once owned by John Gibbons, who in 1849 beat a hasty retreat to America to avoid a poaching charge. California Court now stands on the site. The houses in Belmont Terrace (right) were erected in 1888 and caused an uproar because they infringed the rights to the Downs as common land. Over a hundred years later only the café (to serve bus drivers and conductors at the turn-round) and the very recent houses of Common Side, built over the old coal yard, have been added on that side of the road.

The younger Hennessy children in the garden behind their first home, 13 Downs Road, *c*. 1902. Left to right: Ann (known as Nance), Edie, Jenny, baby Bertie, Jesse. Because of the renumbering of the road (more than once) the exact location of this house is not known, but I believe it to be one of those in the terrace to the east of Clifton Avenue (p. 121). Ernest was the last of the children to be born there, in 1904.

The way across The Downs. This road led directly from Hundred Acre Farm to the railway station (behind the trees), and began as a twin track to accommodate the wheels of horse-drawn carts taking building materials to the mental hospital site. From a distance there is very little change to be seen in the village today.

The introduction of a motor-train service. In 1906, in an attempt to retain passengers who might be attracted by the new-fangled trams, the London, Brighton & South Coast Railway brought in a number of push–pull trains. One feature of these was that the guard, like a tram conductor, issued tickets and used a punch machine. This was worn on a strap slung across one shoulder (as here, during one of the first journeys). Initially the service ran between West Croydon and Belmont. It was extended to Epsom Downs later, but totally withdrawn in 1928. No. 661 was formerly named *Sutton*.

Derby Day crowds, Brighton Road. Annual television coverage of the Epsom Derby has altered public attitudes to the event, so some may now find it more exciting to watch from their own armchairs. Modern transport brings thousands to the racecourse by motorway coach, private car, train and even helicopter. It is hard to understand the fervour that gripped the nation at the turn of the century when the King himself entered horses for the great race. Crowds like this thronged roads leading to and from The Downs, and many more turned out to watch the parade pass by.

Across The Downs. Looking north-west from the general direction of the mental hospital, the Belmont skyline is dominated by the distinctive towers of the South Metropolitan District Schools. Belmont Terrace and the ten cottages on the north side of Downs Road are to the right. Some seventy years later, though the village itself has developed, this stretch of downland remains virtually unaltered. This postcard was printed for R.P. West, stationer and newsagent of Station Road (p. 104).

Station Road, looking east, 1908. These shops and houses are today much as they were over eighty years ago, although the railway station entrance has altered. An iron lattice-construction footbridge over the line, formerly in use at Folkestone Junction, was added immediately north of the road bridge in 1928.

Opposite, bottom: The Creamery and post office, Station Road, 1909. A 1906 directory lists William Henry Brain in charge of Belmont post office in Brighton Road. Within three years it had moved to 4 The Parade. Behind The Creamery were stables where Hodges' delivery carts and horses were kept. Travellers (the equivalent of today's 'reps') were employed to call at houses in the locality for new customers. Miniature portions of butter, cream and milk were left with housewives in the hope that they would be preferred to similar offerings from rival dairies.

Station Road, looking east, from the corner of Belmont Road. This postcard was sent in July 1908 by 'WSH', who was working at the grocers. Until 1884 the Brighton Road bridge farther south and a level crossing at the station were the only links between the communities east and west of the railway line. The local phrase, 'over the bridge', must have begun when this road was opened. The wooden walls and name board of Mr Thomas Jones's coal yard are visible in the centre, with the way to the mental hospital running diagonally towards the horizon, across The Downs.

The Downs Sanatorium gatehouse, Banstead Road, *c.* 1910. When the original South Metropolitan District Schools (p. 82) became overcrowded, six blocks for a separate girls' establishment were built on a large site between Banstead Road (now Cotswold Road) and Downs Road. Over the years the buildings have housed a variety of patients, requiring a considerable number of nursing and domestic staff. The sanatorium also had its own Girl Guide extension company, which was run by Mrs Alice Neate of Pelton Avenue during the Second World War.

Inmates of The Downs School. Part of the sanatorium land is shown on old maps as school grounds. This view appears on a postcard sent on 26 July 1909 by one of the little girls pictured in the garden there.

Greetings from Belmont: the Downs Hospital. 'The Sanny' grew into this large complex of hospital and administrative buildings. In 1963, at a published cost of £1,300,000, it was converted for use as an extension to the Royal Marsden Hospital. Some sources suggest that the Banstead Downs racecourse patronized by King Charles II in the late seventeenth century was first sited near here, but that as time passed Epsom Downs became the favoured position for the sport.

Brighton Road. The arrow-straightness of this road is a reminder of its turnpike days, when Belmont did not exist. The fence of the California tea gardens (centre) marks the boundary of John Gibbons's public house, which received a direct hit in a Second World War air raid. Today the Belmont Carvery and car park cover the whole area. The letter T (far right) is the beginning of a visual reminder to the many visitors to The Downs and the mental hospital that teas and other refreshments awaited them there, as well as at the California.

Downs Road, c. 1910. This illustrates the remarkable fact that at one time Belmont had two 'tin churches' within twelve doors of each other. The 1879 Belmont Mission (far left) was the original of the Free church, which opened in Station Road thirty-six years later. The corrugated iron structure (far right) served as the parish church until the present building was built in 1914. Today the respective sites are occupied by a private house, 37 Downs Road (Bali Hai), and the parish hall, built in 1938.

Avenue Road School, *c*. 1910. Celebrating Empire Day (24 May, instituted in 1877 and commemorating Queen Victoria's birthday), the schoolchildren gather in the playground, watched by the occupants of some of the houses in Kings Road. The staff include Mrs Perry (headmistress), Miss Spence and Miss Rattue. A number of these boys and girls appear in later school groups.

The Conservative Club, 37 Station Road, 1911. King George V and Queen Mary (portrayed above the upstairs windows) were crowned on 22 June of this year. These decorations helped to mark the festivities in the village. On the balcony, left to right: Mrs King, Mrs Hobbs, Mrs Maltby, Mrs Hyder, Mrs Hutchinson, Mrs Russell, Mrs Luxford, Mrs Proudfoot, Mrs Corbett, Mrs Upton, Mrs Chick, Mrs Hilton, Mrs Lovell, Mrs Blake. On the pavement, back row: H. Head, R. Hallett, G. Lovell, J. Blake. Second row, left to right: W. Saunders, E. Tribe, W. Maltby, W. Day, C. Smith, A.H. Hall, A.H. Russell, H.W. Walmisley, Mrs Boniface, Robert Hamilton (photographer), E. Hallett, E. Hyder, W. Simmons. Third row, seated: Revd H.W. Turner, Mrs Walmisley, Mrs Turner. Front row, seated: J. Proudfoot, G. Luxford, J. Burberry, J. Maltby. (Photograph from the Heritage Service Collection, Sutton Central Library.)

Surrey lavender fields, 1910. It is hard to believe that, until building to the west of the railway line began in earnest in the 1880s, fields of lavender, peppermint and strawberries grew in that part of Belmont. There was even a windmill, and cornfields extending towards Cheam.

Avenue Road School, *c*. 1912. The schoolchildren in this playground group include Ernest Alder, Mona Jones and her brother, Cecil Betteridge and his sister, Herbert Westbrook, Phyllis Wilson and her brother, Gladys and Bill Crissell, Phyllis and Hector Burns, Edith and Winifred Washford, Beattie and Minnie Hobbs, and members of the Prosser, George, Pearson and Muggeridge families. The school opened in 1902 and in recent years has become a playgroup centre. A new school has been built farther north on land between Avenue Road and Belmont Rise.

Moving day for the parish church, 1914. A site in the angle of Queens Road, Northdown Road and Belmont Rise having been chosen for the new parish church, the first turf was lifted on 24 June 1914. A ceremony to mark the laying of the foundation stone took place twenty-four days later. This included a symbolic 'removal' from the old site to the new. The head of the procession is by the present 49 Downs Road.

The church of St John the Baptist, 1916. This church was consecrated by the Bishop of Southwark on 23 December 1915, but, before it could be completed to the architect's plan, work was halted and the prospective tower at the west end omitted. Fifty years on, after more than £15,000 had been raised, a meeting room, cloakrooms and kitchen were added, and a nineteenth-century stained-glass window from a demolished Sussex church had been installed. More recently a balcony and two meeting rooms have been added to accommodate Belmont Methodist church, the Station Road premises of which, in serious disrepair, were sold and demolished. A commemorative plaque reads: 'This gallery and the Wesley Rooms were dedicated for God's service on 3 January 1988 by the Rt Rev Ronald Bowlby Bishop of Southwark. They were given by Belmont Methodist Church following the sale of their building in Station Road.' The parish church now bears the unusual title of 'St John's with Belmont Methodists'.

St John's church foundation ceremony, 18 July 1914. Part of the hundred-strong procession is making its way up Station Road to the site of the new church. The land behind the spectators was then part of a nursery garden, but the large hoarding indicates that further building was anticipated. The First World War delayed development of this kind, but work went ahead on the church. The first vicar was Revd Alfred E. Tonkin.

Laying the foundation stone of St John's church. Among the congregation is a small contingent of Boy Scouts (bottom right). Messrs Greenaway & Newberry were appointed as the architects in June 1913, the cost of building having been met by local subscriptions, fund-raising events and donations from neighbouring churches, administered by a building committee. J. Dorey & Co. Limited carried out the work, which was completed in time for the Christmas services in 1915.

The Free church, Station Road. The foundation ceremony took place on Saturday 24 July 1915 and was attended by many local and church dignitaries. Stones were laid (one each side of the entrance) by the pastor of Cheam Baptist church, Mr Arthur Jennings, and by Mrs J. Lees Moffatt, who later became primary superintendent and sick visitor. The church, built on former waste ground where nearby grocer Mr Stapley had kept his delivery horse, was ready for services by 13 November of the same year. In 1928 it became a United Methodist (later Methodist) church. Deacon Court was built on the site after the church moved to the Wesley Rooms in the parish church, which were dedicated in January 1988.

Mr Belcher's greengrocers, 31 Station Road, *c.* 1908. This shop opened in about 1904. It adjoined Mr Stapley's store, the upper floor decorated brick wall of which can also be seen on p. 116. Similar houses were built to the east, and these were only gradually converted into shops. The little girl standing in the shop doorway is Kathleen Belcher (now Mrs London). Today these premises form part of the Conservative Club.

R.P. West, newsagents, Station Road. Some early postcards of Belmont (such as the view across the downs on p. 91, originally a sepia print) were published for Mr West. Rex's in Brighton Road, near the corner of Downs Road, was another shop that issued its own cards. Purchased for a few pennies each and bearing a halfpenny stamp for delivery anywhere inland, they could be sent from Belmont post office (right) or from a pillar box like the one at the Downs Hospital, Banstead Road (p. 94).

The railway station from the bridge, looking north. The rails of the special siding built for the South Metropolitan District Schools (left) were used for more than twenty years from the opening of the line in 1865. They led to the gates, administration building and tree-lined road of the school. The assorted sheds next to the siding belong to Huggett's builders yard (p. 113).

On The Downs, 1913. This postcard was sent on 23 October from Northampton House, Belmont. From the left in the background are some of the village shops, part of the workhouse, the Brighton Road bridge and opening to the goods yard and, behind the central telegraph pole, the large white corner shop at the junction of Downs Road and Brighton Road. The tank locomotive waiting to back into the yard is thought to be a Stroudley 'D' or 'E' class, but several important clues to identification are obscured by the gorse bushes. (Thanks to Mr Alan Jones of Seaford Museum railway model group for detailed technical advice.)

Burdon Lane, 1915. This lane, believed to be named after a stream that once flowed along the same course, was originally a much longer track. It ran from Woodmansterne in the south, crossing the London to Brighton road and continuing north to the London to Epsom road. The angled junction with Brighton Road (near the golf course) was a dangerous intersection, not helped by a grass-covered reservoir on one corner partially obstructing the motorist's view south. In the late 1960s official approval was given for the end of the lane to be blocked off, leaving the exit from Belmont Rise, a few yards to the north, as the only access in that area.

Banstead Downs Golf Club, 1920s–30s. This club was founded for ladies in October 1890, but gentlemen were admitted to membership within the year. The club moved to the present Burdon Lane site in 1899 from its original tin hut near Banstead Railway Cottages. A lounge and putting green were added in 1923, and major development took place in the 1960s. The short section of Burdon Lane between the clubhouse and Brighton Road (in the foreground) has since been sealed off.

Pupils of Banstead Road Council School, 1916. Back row, left to right: Phyllis Wilson, Stella Pope, Elsie Slater, Florence Dobell, Raymond Day, Ernest Alder, Frederick Streeter, Frederick Clowser. Second row: Mona Jones, Gladys Hardwick, Minnie Hobbs, Connie Chambers, Rose Hyder, Edna Froude, Beatie ?, Annie Cooper, Ethel Osgood, Mr Ashton (headmaster). Third row: Violet Cummings, Edith Washford, Olive Shepherd, Beattie Hobbs, Ethel Pope, Gladys Crissell, Cecil Carpenter, Gus Shepherd. Front row: Stanley Hook, Ernest Hennessy, T. Steele, Arthur Paxton. Teachers at the school included Miss Lucy Parker and Miss Sawyer. My mother recalled all these names nearly eighty years on.

The Hennessy boys, *c.* 1919. William Junior ('Bill') and Jesse (standing, left and right) fought in the First World War, but Ernest, the youngest of the family, was only ten years old when the war began. After the Armistice Jesse joined the Merchant Navy and emigrated. Bill, who had served in France with the 8th East Surrey Regiment, was employed by the local electricity company, the JEA. Ernie left school a few days before his fourteenth birthday to work as a lab boy at the Belmont Laboratories in Ventnor Road. After nineteen months he was taken on by Dr J.W. Dalgleish of Grove Road, Sutton, as motor boy. He eventually joined his brother Bill at the JEA.

3 Banstead Road,

Belmont,

Surrey.

November 11th, 1918.

My Dear Dada.,

Just a few lines as I have a little time to spare. I have not written to you for such a long time, that I must now while I have the chance. Well, at last the war is over. Everybody is so pleased that they are getting drunk over it. The children and Winnie and I went down to Sutton Station to see the sights, and all the soldiers were rolling about and singing. Everyone was wearing red white and blue ribbon and the children were carrying small flags. The soldiers in the War Hospital(our men I mean) were marching round the building and playing the band, waving the Allies Flags. There never was such a day as this, November 11th. It will always be a Bank-Holiday after this as the 4th August is. Well, I think you will soon be home for good. To read the paper there seems a good amount of work to have been going on at the War-Office lately. In tonights paper it said what the men were going to have given them when they were released. It is good, as I expect you will say. We must cheer up and have a little more patience now the war is over and see what comes of it.

Well, I am pleased to say I am better from the Flu. It was horrid, I dont want it again. Hughie is better too. In the paper it said the epidemic was less severe. I hope it will soon die out.

I have just heard the church bells ringing, the first I have heard for long time. There wont be any fireworks on account of the rain, but the boys have been promised that they shall stay up to see them when they are up. Well I must close now,

With Love From. Your Affectionate Daughter

Edie. xxx xxxx

Rex's Corner, Brighton Road/Downs Road, looking north. Most features of this view speak for themselves, from the No. 164 bus advertising *The Great Pop Mystery* (still unsolved?) to the 'Stop me and buy one' trade cycle attended by the Wallsie (purveyor of Walls ice-cream). The latter's wares included a Snofrute (similar to an iced lolly) at 1d., a 1d. or 2d. cornet, a tub, sold with a small, flat wooden spoon, and a 2d. wafer, which was a miniature vanilla block sandwiched between two thin biscuits. The shop was built in 1888, near The California Arms (opposite the inn sign), which had been in existence for some years. Both belonged to the Gibbons family, and it was one of their descendants who gave his name to Pelton Avenue, at the far side of the inn.

Opposite: The end of the First World War, 11 November 1918. This eye-witness account of armistice celebrations sent to her soldier father by Edith Washford was typewritten during her secretarial class that evening at Sutton Public Hall. The 'flu' to which she refers was one of several influenza epidemics that claimed many lives about that time. It is ironic that rain spoiled some celebrations of the end of the First World War – on VE Day 1945 (the end of the war in Europe), too, people walked to the highest point on Belmont Downs, hoping to see London's lights go on again, but all was shrouded in drizzle.

A wedding at the Free church, 1920s. When the new church was completed in November 1915, the first president (pastor) was Mr R.P. Smith. The next permanent president, who served the church for ten years, was Mr Alfred Day. On his leaving in 1928 the decision was made to join the United Methodist church in the Thornton Heath circuit. The Revd Luke Hicks was Belmont's first Methodist minister. (Photograph from the collection of Mrs Kath London.)

Girls' Friendly Society, *c.* 1921. Members of the local GFS performed *Snow White and Rose Red*. In costume for the play are, left to right, Edith Washford, Sarah Richardson and Winifred Washford. The group sometimes met at Belmont vicarage.

J. Huggett & Son, builders, 1920s. This group of buildings is featured in photographs of the railway station area. They stood near the entrance to the road leading to the South Metropolitan Schools. The buildings included the office (above), the paint shed and other workshops (below). A garage and petrol station on the east corner of Belmont Road also belonged to J. Huggett & Son.

The cottage hospital. Succeeding a small hospital in Bushey Road (near the gasworks), this building, given by Mr Passmore Edwards, was completed in 1902. The site in Hill Road, Sutton, was donated by Sir Ralph C. Forster. Eventually the hospital had thirty-two beds, but these were not enough for the rapidly expanding community so a fresh start had to be made.

Overton's Farm, c. 1925. My uncles Hugh and Henley, and aunts Lilian and Violet Washford, with two older friends, were picnicking in the field where, in 1930, Sutton and Cheam Hospital would be built. At the end of the First World War a tented army camp was in this field. When the soldiers left, Brenda, the Washford family's Airedale dog, went with them. Probably army rations were better than those of civilians.

The foundations of Sutton and Cheam General Hospital, Banstead Road, 1930. This hospital was built in the field shown opposite (below) to a design by William Pite Son & Fairweather. Left to right: Ernest Hennessy and his baby daughter, Pat, Henley and Elsie Washford (behind) and their daughters Lilian and Violet.

Sutton and Cheam General Hospital. The hospital was opened on 30 September 1931 by Sir Alan Garrett Anderson, KBE, on the south-east corner of Banstead Road (now Cotswold Road) and Chiltern Road. It originally accommodated twenty-two male, twenty-two female, twelve children and twelve private patients. The nurses' home is in the centre.

A later view of Station Road. The Methodist church hall (behind the telegraph pole) was founded in 1926, originally to accommodate the increasingly popular Sunday School, during the ministry of Revd Alfred Day. On the east corner of Kings Road (far right) is Stapley's shop, today part of the Constitutional Club premises. The trees (left) mark the edge of the nursery gardens and field where 32 and 34 Station Road and the telephone exchange would be built.

Station Road, looking west, 1930s. The Schweppes lorry is probably making a delivery to Tonge's (No. 6), which sold ales and soft drinks as well as groceries. The lorry on the right belongs to greengrocer Tommy Green and is parked outside his shop, which has goods on display on the pavement. The striped sunblind is over the window of Pratt's the sweetshop, and businesses beyond Green's include a hairdresser and a filling station.

Lionel Tertis, CBE, LRAM. This celebrated musician started his career at the age of thirteen as pianist with a 'Hungarian' band in Scarborough. Seven years later he began playing the viola, the cause of which he championed for the rest of his life. In about 1909 he and his wife, Ada, came to live in Belmont at Smalldown, 63 The Crescent. In the First World War he served as a special constable. His duties included guarding the Ventnor Road reservoir, where he was able to fit in some practice. My mother remembers hearing the music of his viola as she walked up Brighton Road on her way home from evening classes. On retirement in 1937 Mr Tertis left Belmont, but he resumed recitals in 1940 to raise funds for war charities. He died in 1975 in his ninety-ninth year.

Avenue Road, 1930s. The photographer stood near the gate of 3 Avenue Road to get this view of the bungalows on the east side. Stand in the same spot today and it is easy to identify the same houses, although the removal of bushes and fences has opened up the aspect most attractively. The increase in the volume of traffic, however, makes it difficult to catch such a peaceful glimpse.

Belmont Road, March 1920. A group of young cyclists has paused to be photographed on vacant land near the corner of Station Road. Behind them is the end wall of 2 Belmont Road, and on the left is a glimpse of Nos 5 and 7. Straddling the Brighton Road, Belmont was on a direct route to the Surrey woods – countryside within pedalling distance of south London. It was common on spring Sunday evenings between the two world wars to see these groups cycling north, homeward bound, with huge bunches of cowslips or bluebells fastened behind their saddles.

Kings Road, looking north, 1930s. At the far end of the road is Cross Road, leading (on the right) into Belmont Road. Beyond is the boundary fence of the old South Metropolitan District Schools, usually known locally as 'the workhouse'. The houses on the right run in one continuous terrace, pierced only by an arched passageway leading to the back of the properties, the position of which is marked by a single gable breaking the straight roof line. The building of the schools began in about 1852, and some of Belmont's earliest residential development, for the schools' personnel, was in the Kings Road and Belmont Road area.

Conservative Club outing, *c.* 1932. Arthur Perrin, Lily Mitchell, Jim Perrin and members of the Paxton family are among those about to board the coach outside the club premises at 37 Station Road. This was the earlier headquarters, before the club moved to the east corner of Queens Road.

Holland Avenue, looking north, 1930s. The noticeboard of the lawn tennis club is among the bushes (right). The club continues to occupy the same ground. Behind the houses (left) were the South Metropolitan District Schools, most recently occupied by Henderson Hospital and now being demolished to make way for residential development.

The Atora covered wagon, 1934. Drawn by two bullocks, wagons like this delivered Hugon's Atora beef suet ('shredded for puddings, pie crust, mincemeat . . . blocks for frying fish and potatoes') between 1893 and the early part of the Second World War. Atora suet has survived, and the present manufacturers, RHM Foods Limited, say: 'This turned out to be one of the best publicity stunts run by a nationally known firm. Later the wagons joined Chipperfield's Circus and took part in parades up and down the country.' The wagon stopped in Station Road outside Mr Jones's drapery, on the corner of The Crescent.

Belmont Downs, 1937. Cousins Violet Washford (back), Shirley Fuller (left), Pat Hennessy (right) and John Washford (front) on one of the tracks leading from Rex's Corner to Banstead Mental Hospital. In the background are, left to right: 79 Downs Road (on the corner of Clifton Avenue) and the terrace including 81 to 93 Downs Road.

Downs Road, 1936. Mrs Jane Hennessy (née Cleall) is standing in the back garden of her home at 41 Downs Road. Earlier this same house was known as 2 Downs Road, 2 The Downs and 2 Downland Cottages. The distant houses are in Pelton Avenue, and the tall chimney seems to be part of neighbour Miss Fowler's garden shed!

Alderman Sir Sidney Marshall, DL, MP, JP. Sir Sidney's home was Bracklin, The Crescent, now demolished and replaced by Patricia Gardens. He was a county alderman, Charter Mayor of Sutton and Cheam in 1934, and the first member for the borough constituency created eleven years later. He died in 1973 in his ninetieth year, having been concerned in innumerable ways with St John's church from 1921, when first elected to the parochial church council.

The Boys' Brigade, 1938. In this year the Belmont group was awarded (left to right) the athletics, drill, football, swimming and physical training shields.

The three editors of the Boys' Brigade, c. 1937. At this time the Belmont group had their own magazine. Left to right: George Rex, Leslie Perrin, Bruce White.

Sutton Training Centre, 1939. The South Metropolitan District Schools closed after nearly forty years' service. From 1908 until 1939, with a break in the First World War when German prisoners of war were kept there, the buildings were used as a workhouse. During the Second World War the buildings became a rehabilitation centre. This postcard was one of a series published by E.F. Brown of 28 Station Road.

Brighton Road, looking north, 1930s. Behind the hedge (left) was open ground down to the railway line, until the building of the 'prefabs' (prefabricated single-storey homes put up to ease the post-war housing shortage). These have since been replaced by Hulverston Close, Yarbridge Close and others. The fence and bushes (right) mark the extent of a large area of allotments, bounded on the east by Cotswold Road. Where the two roads meet (in the distance) stood an imposing drinking fountain. In the Second World War a public air raid shelter was made nearby, inside the lower gate of the allotments. One day a neat round hole appeared in the road by the fountain with a flimsy barrier around it, which did not deter people from peering in. The following day we heard that an unexploded bomb had made the hole and was lying at the bottom.

Inside The California, 1943. This public house suffered major damage, and a number of lives were lost in one of Belmont's worst incidents in the Second World War when an enemy bomb scored a direct hit. The surviving part of the premises was repaired and put back in service. I can remember the stunted little building that carried the old name until redevelopment and expansion resulted in today's Belmont Carvery. Left to right: Mr F. Weylan, Mr Arthur Perrin, Mr G. Carr.

The entrance block, Belmont Hospital. Although a number of bombs fell harmlessly on The Downs and on other open ground during the Second World War, others caused damage and loss of life. The prominent buildings of the hospital were an easy target, and nearby homes suffered broken windows and the effects of blast. Several internal disasters have also threatened the hospital. Beginning in 1856, only a few weeks after the homeless children were moved in, the buildings have caught fire several times over the years.

Station Road in the Second World War. Signs of the times include the delivery bike at the kerb by Brown's the newsagents. Dick Isted is standing in the doorway of the newsagents. Hayter's was one of two village grocery stores, where my family was registered for rationed items of food. The other was Tonge's at 6 Station Road. The shop with blank windows (above Hayter's) served a number of wartime purposes: as the local Auxiliary Fire Service centre, and later when Wing Commander Lee-Rayner displayed a famous carrier pigeon, which had been awarded the Deakin Medal for battle services.

A wartime view of Station Road. Blackout precautions seen here include the white markings on the kerbs, and on the running-board and bumper of the car. On the opposite corner of Belmont Road (off the picture, right) was the garage requisitioned by the local Auxiliary Fire Service (later the NFS). The fireman with a gasmask haversack is on picket duty.

1st Belmont Girl Guides, 1944. Poppy, Shamrock and Forget-me-not partrols are parading in the playground of Avenue Road School for inspection. Those present include Joyce Mills, Joyce Williams, Pam Mills, Pat Hennessy, Pat Cooper, Ann Bawtree, Barbara Carter (holding mascot, 'Katy'), Audrey van der Vord, Eileen Cook, Anne Roynon, Barbara Pearce and Lieutenant Teresa Fortescue, who is carrying out the inspection.

Victory celebration, 1945. Victory in Europe (VE) was marked by hanging out all available patriotic flags. Food was still rationed and non-essentials were hard to find. Matters had improved by the time our armed forces returned to be 'demobbed', so 'Welcome Home' parties were well-organized, colourful events.

Welcome Home Dinner, Shinner's Restaurant, Sutton, 1947. After the Second World War a number of events were held for local servicemen and women returning to 'Civvy Street'. The diners include Miss Win Cox, Mr & Mrs John Day, Miss Eileen Dunn, ? Elliott, Miss Halsted, Mr & Mrs Hedges, Mrs Kath London, Mr & Mrs Mansell, Miss Bobby Murray, Mr & Mrs Jack Page (née Maradel Voss), Mr & Mrs Les Perrin, Bill ('Tubby') Ward and John Worker.

The Boys Brigade. The number of members rose after the Second World War. This group includes Leslie Perrin (in raincoat), Benny Thurgood (with Union flag), Colin Worker, John London and Bill Burtwell.

St. JOHN'S CHURCH PARISH HALL
DOWNS ROAD, BELMONT

THE CHOIR

presents

THE HARRISON CARTER CHAMBER ORCHESTRA

with

MARY JARRED
(Contralto)

and

MERLE-MARY BARNES
(Solo Violin)

on Saturday, 7th June

at 8 p.m.

IN AID OF CHURCH CHOIR ROBES

PROGRAMME — — SIXPENCE

Banstead Mental Hospital. A large staff of attendants and domestic workers was needed to care for the many patients, and in the 1950s they had an active social club. At Christmas the St John's church choir visited some of the wards to sing carols.

Opposite: A programme for a concert at St John's Parish Hall, 1947. The church choir had been depleted during the Second World War, so the organist and choirmaster, Mr William Bigsby, recruited more than thirty girl singers from local schools and from the church fellowship choral group. In spite of fund-raising events like this concert, there were not enough new blue robes for all of the girls and they were formed into two units. When the full choir was needed some of the members appeared in mufti. A robing vestry for the girls was contrived in the organ loft.

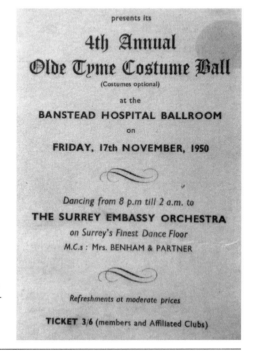

presents its

4th Annual
Olde Tyme Costume Ball
(Costumes optional)

at the

BANSTEAD HOSPITAL BALLROOM

on

FRIDAY, 17th NOVEMBER, 1950

Dancing from 8 p.m till 2 a.m. to
THE SURREY EMBASSY ORCHESTRA
on Surrey's Finest Dance Floor
M.C.s : Mrs. BENHAM & PARTNER

Refreshments at moderate prices

TICKET 3/6 (members and Affiliated Clubs)

Advertisement for a costume ball, 1950. The hospital social club included an old-time group, whose grand dances attracted many guests and top orchestras.

St John's parish hall, 4 May 1949. Members of the Church Youth Fellowship are performing *Orange Blossom*. Those present include Sheila Cooper, Sheila O'Clarey, Ron Morris, Ray Tulley, Pat Hennessy and Yvonne Howard. The adult leaders of this Fellowship were Mr and Mrs A. Wolfe.

The Crescent, from the gateway of No. 40, 1930s. The road curves gently north towards the shopping centre. At the turn of the century it was sometimes called Crescent Road. It was one of the village's first residential developments, with imposing mansions built for leading citizens and businessmen, the early commuters. In about 1904, here and in Northdown and Queens Roads, trees were planted by Mr Alfred Belcher for the estate owners. Families living there during the Second World War included the Harts, whose son John and daughter Jean were professional dancers, and the Judds, whose daughter Agnes (Nancy) was my Nonsuch schoolfellow and son Frank was made a baron in 1991.

Street party, June 1953. A vast fancy-dress party for village children was organized in the Belmont Road/Cross Road/Kings Road area to celebrate the coronation of Queen Elizabeth II.

Street party, June 1953. No doubt many good citizens now aged forty-five and over will be able to identify themselves among the fairy tale characters, cowboys, pirates and princesses joining in the celebrations.

Mrs E. Hennessy at the door of 5A Cotswold Road, 1951. During the Second World War building materials were diverted from residential projects to munition factories and service establishments. Many existing homes were damaged or destroyed in air raids. In the resulting housing shortage even small, semi-detached cottages were subdivided. No. 5's front door led directly by staircase to the upper flat, and the original back door, looking onto the yard, became the entrance to the lower flat, 5A.

St John the Baptist church, 1950s. This view is from the stone cross monument in memory of Belmont men and women lost in two world wars. The church looks much as it did at its dedication in 1915. Since the 1950s the major external change at this end of the building is the clock above the central window, added to commemorate the Queen's Silver Jubilee in 1977.

Cornwall Road, from the south-west corner of Northey Avenue, looking diagonally across Belmont Rise, 1930s. This view has plenty of features to allow the identification of the same houses today.

York Road, running parallel with Cornwall Road to the east, marks the course of an ancient north–south cattle track to The Downs from the London Road, the continuation of a track that became Gander Green Lane.

No. 41 Downs Road, 1966. This house was the Hennessy family home from about 1906, when William and Jane moved with their children from a cottage some distance farther along Downs Road. Miss Ann Hennessy ('Nance') lived the rest of her life here after her seven brothers and sisters moved on. For many years, including the whole of the Second World War, she served newspapers, sweets and cigarettes to the customers of Browns at 28 Station Road, 'over the bridge'.

The station, looking south, 1960s. Under the iron footbridge, brought from Folkestone in 1928 and removed again some sixty years later, and under the road bridge immediately alongside, is a glimpse of the Brighton Road bridge. The Down platform buildings were demolished by an enemy bomb in 1940. No such reasonable explanation has been given for the condition of the Up side. The line was singled for the first time in its 117-year history in 1982, and bushes have grown to cover the whole of the area on the right.

Sister Jean Johnson. Sister Johnson lived at 39 Kings Road. She received her decoration as a member of the Order of the British Empire at Buckingham Palace, in recognition of her services to nursing and, in particular, of her relief work in Yugoslavia after a massive earthquake in 1963.

Browns the newsagents, 1969. From 28 Station Road this shop moved to No. 24. The proprietor was Harold Heyes (left). Nigel Taylor is in the doorway. In my mother's day this was May's the shoe shop, but I remember it as Mr Greer's café and cake shop. In spite of wartime shortages there were usually home-made scones and cakes for sale, with pleasant cooking aromas wafting into the shop from the kitchen.

The Avenue Primary School, *c*. 1956. Avenue Road School catered for the younger children of the village (p. 99) until a site between Avenue Road and Belmont Rise was chosen for a new school (above). The first two classrooms were built by September 1956. Although the infants' department stayed on in the old premises for a time, children in both groups have been accommodated at the new school for over twenty years. Sir Sidney Marshall (below) of Bracklin, The Crescent, addresses the children and their guests. Seen through the windows are the new green playing fields that have replaced their old cramped schoolyard.

The teaching swimming pool, The Avenue School. The building of this pool began in 1958 and the official opening took place in June 1959.

The members of Class 8, The Avenue Primary School, July 1962.

The Avenue Primary School. On District Sports Day, 3 July 1963, these young pupils won the Small Schools (Boys) Shield.

Fund-raising event for The Avenue Primary School pool shelter. An original idea was this stop-watch competition. Left to right: Mr Elbourne (manager of Westminster Bank, Cheam), Mrs Elbourne, Mrs Moore, Councillor Moore (chairman of the school managers and honorary treasurer of the pool fund). Mr Moore died in May 1974, only a few months before work on the shelter began.

The Avenue Primary School pool shelter. Jumble sales, sponsored walks, fairs and a talk by Professor James Blades, the celebrated percussionist, helped to raise money for the shelter. Parents worked 774 man-hours on the installation between September and December 1974.

SECTION SEVEN

Banstead

Banstead crossroads, early 1930s. The far arm of the signpost indicates the eastward section of today's A2022 Winkworth Road (centre). The village of Banstead lies uphill through the trees (right). Near here was a tennis-court on which, in the late 1940s, members of St John's Youth Fellowship, Belmont, had permission to play. Traffic-lights were installed at the crossroads in 1936 as the volume of traffic on the Brighton road increased.

Cuddington Golf Club, 1930s. The course, originally of 6,472 yards, is situated on the lower slopes of Banstead Downs, in a roughly triangular area enclosed by Banstead Road, Cuddington Way and the boundary with Banstead Downs Golf Course to the east. Both course (designed by H.S. Colt) and clubhouse opened on 1 January 1929. The horizontal line of low bushes marks Banstead Road, which has to be crossed to play holes 7, 8 and 9. The tenth hole is played from a point behind the two parked cars. The clubhouse was designed with a billiard room, lounge and dance floor, cocktail bar and restaurant, and a ladies' lounge.

Windmill Bridge, Banstead Downs, 1930s. This rustic bridge spans the cutting on the Belmont–Banstead section of the railway line opened in May 1865 by the London, Brighton & South Coast Railway. It carries one of the old bridle paths which have crossed The Downs for many years. The mounds of soil displaced by gangs of navigators ('navvies') digging the cutting were left showing white and became known locally as 'the chalk hills'. In Domesday (1086) Banstead, 'held by Richard', is recorded as having a mill.

High Street, looking east, *c.* 1914. At the T-junction by the long brick wall the horse and cart would have turned right into Park Road or Woodmansterne Lane leading to open farmland and downs, or left into Sutton Lane, now the B2218. The latter has remained mercifully undeveloped, overlooked only by Banstead Mental Hospital and its recent successor, the prison.

The Old Well and Park Road, 1911. It is recorded that this well, when in use, was 300 feet deep. This postcard was produced for Tonge's, the High Street grocer not far from this junction. In 1944 people were killed and injured and buildings in the area badly damaged when a bomb fell nearby.

The High Street, 1940s. The same tall tree in these opposite views marks the former site of the village pond. The building with its end wall exposed (above) is 107 High Street. The picture below was drawn for the Ibis Library, which is featured in the drawing and still remains in the High Street. The vehicle is parked at the kerb by the village school, which was demolished in 1992 to make way for a Waitrose store.

All Saints' church. It is probable that a church has occupied this site for 1,200 years. One is recorded for the twenty-eight villagers and fifteen cottagers who, with seven slaves, made up the population of Banstead when Domesday was compiled. The present church contains many features surviving from the twelfth and thirteenth centuries, though major alterations took place during Victorian times. Within living memory interior wall-paintings and texts have been whitewashed over.

The vicarage, 1912. The occupant at this time was the Revd D. Woodroffe, MA. The list of vicars goes back to Ranulph in 1282. It was during the ministry of the Revd E.V. Buckle, MA (the third of that surname to be vicar of Banstead), that the notable west window was installed. Made at the William Morris works, it was designed by Pre-Raphaelite artist Dante Gabriel Rossetti.

The Revd Frederick Schofield, 1959. Mr Schofield was vicar from 1954 to 1972, a time of great change in and around Banstead as post-war expansion got under way. Major restoration of the church roof took place during his ministry. The memorial tablet on the wall behind him is one of a number bearing the family name of the Lamberts who, together with the Buckles and the de Burghs, served the church for many generations.

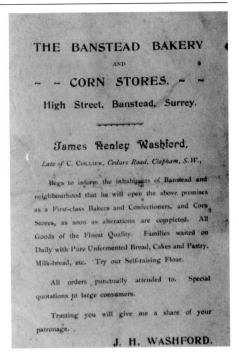

Advertisement for The Banstead Bakery and Corn Stores. From about 1907 my grandfather practised his skills as a baker and confectioner in Banstead village, numbering families, schools and hospitals among his customers. His wife, Elsie, served in the shop and kept the accounts. My grandfather continued the decorative icing of wedding, birthday and other cakes as a hobby, long after his retirement.

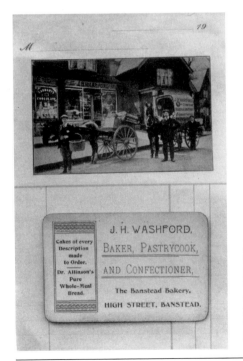

J.H. Washford, The Banstead Bakery. This shop stood in the High Street opposite the pond (which was drained in 1929 when the shops on that side were developed). Access to the bakehouse was through the passage (centre). Mr Balchin, the saddler, also had premises there. Assisting my grandfather (centre) was his younger brother, Walter (left).

The grounds of Garratts Hall. The family name of Garratt goes back more than five hundred years to Thomas Gerard, who was recorded as the chief landowner in Banstead, 'the place where beans are grown'. By the end of the sixteenth century the spelling of the name had changed to Garrard. The last owners of the old house and surrounding estate were the Lambert family, for whom my grandmother worked as a girl. Garratts Hall was demolished in about 1933.

A family picnic, *c*. 1910. Left to right: Mrs Dalrymple (whose husband took the photograph), Mrs Elsie Washford, Miss Edie Washford, Master Willie Dalrymple, Mrs Elsie Grant, Miss Winnie Washford, Mr Henley Washford. Smart clothes and picnic fare, with a large stone jar of ginger beer, seem a world away from today's barbecues.

Rose Hill School, Park Road. This house dates from 1770. Formerly known as The Rook's Nest, it took its school name from a nearby farm. In 1966 the firm of Galliford Seear occupied the building and called it Castle House after the motif of the company badge. (Thanks to Mr Levine of Galliford Seear for this information.)

Oaks Hill, Woodmansterne. Oaks Hill is possibly the eastern extremity of the original Burdon Lane (p. 106). The Oaks Park has now been made into an extensive golf course and leisure centre, but Lord Derby's country seat of the same name, where the idea was born for 'the blue riband of the turf', has not survived.

Lych-gate and memorial, Woodmansterne. The area appears in Domesday as Odemerestor. It had a church even then.

Chipstead church. Chipstead appears in Domesday, and in the list of its people and land a mill is mentioned. A few timbered farmhouses and cottages can still be found in the countryside. Part of this church dates from the thirteenth century. It was rebuilt nearly five hundred years later.

Chipstead and Banstead Downs station. In 1890 Mr Cosmo Bonsor of Kingswood Warren, sometime general manager of the South East and Chatham Railway, sought the convenience of a train station near his home. Lengthy negotiations ensued between the various railway companies operating in the area. The Chipstead Valley line to Tattenham Corner was agreed on, with an eye to racegoers' demands. Chipstead and Banstead Downs station opened on 2 November 1897. The station at Tadworth and Walton-on-the-Hill opened three years later. The line first carried Derby Day crowds on 4 June 1901. 'Banstead Downs' has since been dropped from the title. The station was closed to goods on 7 May 1962. (Additional information kindly supplied by Mr Maurice Finch of Seaford.)

Banstead Road South. Banstead Road runs from north to south for more than a mile and a half, from Park Hill, Carshalton, to Downs Road, Belmont. The section below the junction with The Crossways was designated Banstead Road South when it was developed across Overton's farmland.

The Beeches. How beautiful and beloved these trees must have been for the London, Brighton & South Coast Railway to commemorate them in the name of their new station in 1906. Beeches Halt became Carshalton Beeches station in 1925 when the West Croydon to Epsom Downs line was electrified. Little Holland House, with exhibits from the Arts and Crafts Movement, is a historic house in Beeches Avenue and is open to the public.

Beeches Walk. This short road winds gently downhill from Banstead Road South, with glimpses through the trees of the Wellfield Plantation and the vast complex of Queen Mary's Children's Hospital.

Pine Walk, near Belmont. A favourite stroll when I lived in Furzedown Road, Belmont, this road curves north-east from Banstead Road South towards The Warren, with views towards The Oaks Park, which has since been developed as a sports complex. So our nostalgic journey through some well-loved Surrey villages draws gently to a close.

Acknowledgements

While this book is based on a lifetime's recollections of two beloved villages, it has been necessary to update and enhance my records. For help in this I thank the following, not already mentioned: Jeremy Harte and the staff at Bourne Hall Museum; Alison Kearns and the staff at Sutton Heritage Centre; Mr & Mrs Beattie and Mr Noel Bibby of St Andrew's church, Northey Avenue; Mrs Kath London, John and Daphne London, and Mr Harold Heyes (for help, hospitality and the loan of photographs); Mrs Barbara Edser and Pamela; Professor John White and the staff of the Royal Academy of Music; Mrs Janie Perrin of Belmont; Mr Maurice Finch of Seaford; Mr Patel of Belmont post office; the Secretary of Cuddington Golf Club; Mrs V. Barkey, headmistress of Nonsuch County School for Girls; Mrs Hilda Bristow of Ewell; my old schoolfriend Miss Audrey Seeley, without whose support I would not have moved very fast or done much lateral thinking.

Facts have to be checked, and to do so I consulted *Splendid the Heritage* by C. Leslie Craig, *A Village Church* by Margaret Reed, *History of the Southern Railway* by Michael R. Bonavia, *West Croydon to Epsom* by Vic Mitchell & Keith Smith, *Cinderella no More* by Lionel Tertis, Mr Frank Burgess's Sutton Leisure Services picture books and *Banstead Downs Golf Club: the First Hundred Years* by Alfred King.

Among those pictures reproduced, none appears to be under copyright, but the current practice of marketing photographic copies means that the original details from their backs are not available. Apologies are rendered for any source not fully cleared or acknowledged.